MEMPHIS
SWEET, SPICY & A LITTLE GREASY

34 CHEFS SUPPORT THE ARTS WITH FRESH FARE AND RAW TALENT

MEMPHIS
SWEET, SPICY & A LITTLE GREASY

SUSAN SCHADT

WITH ANNIE BARES

PHOTOGRAPHS BY LISA BUSER

FOREWORD BY CHEF KELLY ENGLISH

LIMITED EDITION
BENEFITTING ArtsMemphis
WILD ABUNDANCE™ PUBLISHING 2014

Kendall Britt, Ballet Memphis Company member

TABLE OF CONTENTS

FOREWORD

CHEF KELLY ENGLISH

Memphis to me is about a collective spirit that belongs to none of us and all of us at the same time. We are all a part of something much greater than our individual businesses or ourselves; we are part of a real community that cares deeply about itself. We are not perfect, we are not new and shiny, and we do not need to be nor want to be any of that. I look at a place like Earnestine and Hazel's and it says so much to me about this town: the floors are cracked, the walls are broken and littered with signs spelled phonetically, and the bathtubs upstairs don't work anymore. But the beer is cold, the soul burgers are hot all night, the jukebox is unparalleled, the people there are celebrating life…this is what matters, and here in Memphis, what matters is always special.

On these pages you will find the work of ArtsMemphis and the vision of Susan Schadt, viewed through the lens of Lisa Buser and told by the folks that I have the privilege to call colleagues. When we first talked about the series, we knew we wanted to have collaborations between chefs, artists, musicians, and performers in nontraditional spots to make completely unique parties. The diversity in the groupings was important to us, because the story of Memphis has so much to do with the diversity in all kinds of things: race, religion, music, food, and the list goes on and on. And the struggle for us to get to where we are today makes us who we are right now. Each of these parties was a collective vision that was arrived at by many different vantage points of each individual involved.

When you flip around in this story, you will see a very strong common theme: people are genuinely having a great deal of fun. Some events were about bubbles in champagne, some were about bubbles in cheap beer, but they all were about sharing these truly special evenings with each other. Because these dinners were so much fun to put on, I know I can speak for everyone when I say that we wanted to plan the next year right away. I have been back to Earnestine and Hazel's a few times since the night of our party, and the scene each time has been littered with people dancing, people sobering up with a burger or having just one more and I think "this is perfect too."

Cheers

2009 *Food & Wine Magazine "Best New Chef,"* Kelly English is executive chef/owner of acclaimed Restaurant Iris and The Second Line in Memphis. He was a 2010 James Beard Award nominee for Best Chef: Southeast.

Chefs Kelly English, Patrick Reilly and Jason Severs

PREFACE

SUSAN SCHADT

Each year ArtsMemphis features a signature artist whose work informs and inspires the theme of our culinary series. For our 2013 series, *Beauty and the Feast*, the artist was Memphian Tad Lauritzen Wright. His painting, *Into the Pink*, and the tagline he imagined, "Love on the Installment Plan" was a dish we were ready to serve up hot-out-of-the-oven.

With the mere utterance of a second culinary arts dinner series to support the arts in Memphis, the magic began. Hands went up all over town. The first call was to Kelly English, Chair of our Culinary Arts Advisory Council. Before we knew it, we had thirty-four chefs from four states forming teams. They were mixing food, passion and the gift of their time and talent to develop menus and events with grit and grace — Memphis style.

When fully baked, potential complications were overcome by an advanced course in "Community". ArtsMemphis board member, Greg Baudoin spearheaded the series for the second consecutive year and was joined by his co chair, stylist Mimsie Crump. Combine a very generous donation of a design "dream team" from Wimmer Companies, a local firm nationally renowned as the country's premier cookbook printer; add the flawless execution and untold hours by ArtsMemphis staff; mix well. The result was the makings for twelve incredible *Installments* and the ultimate lagniappe, a book celebrating our great city.

The rare photographic glimpse into our city captured in these pages by Lisa Buser's artistic eye, sings as soulfully as Blind Mississippi Morris' harmonica, the Bo-Keys quintessential Memphis Sound and Valerie June's harmonies. The images reflect tradition and changing appetites. Lisa and her camera are storytellers — Southern style.

This book is the second publication I have worked on with Annie Bares, an ArtsMemphis colleague. The first was *A Million Wings* in 2012 when she was at Rhodes College and an intern for ArtsMemphis. We traveled across the country interviewing business titans, all duck hunters. Luckily, Annie is from Lafayette, Louisiana, so she gets all this frenzy around hunting and food. She has been an integral part of this book and, despite her youth, a touchstone for me. She also knows how to interview, transcribe, write and laugh — Louisiana style.

The arts groups, artists, chefs, hosts, stylists, and vendors created events that gave guests a taste of the authentic, creative, cultural currency that is all our own. All but a soupçon of this collective commitment was either gifted, donated or volunteered. From the unpolished to the refined, the blues to ballet, food trucks to fine dining, this series of *Installments* revels in our city's one-of-a-kind spirit, serves up over seventy chefs' recipes, imaginative entertaining tips and is forever chronicled in *MEMPHIS: Sweet, Spicy & a Little Greasy*.

L to r: Lee Plesofsky, Margaret Ledbetter, Greg Baudoin, Lucia Heros

BE NICE OR LEAVE

NEW ORLEANS AND MEMPHIS SHARE A SPECIAL KINSHIP. The first and second busiest port cities on the Mississippi River, they have played prominent roles in the history of American commerce and culture. From the blues and barbeque to brass bands and beignets, both cities have left us with inspiring legacies of music and food. Be Nice or Leave was an unforgettable ode to the exchange of food, music and friends between these two one-of-a-kind cities.

The home of hosts Lucia and Ricky Heros provided the perfect setting for a New Orleans-themed brunch, styled by Memphis interior designer Greg Baudoin who transformed the Heros' Chickasaw Gardens home into the iconic Garden District style for the party. Guests arrived to find the entry gate strewn with Mardi Gras beads, a scene reminiscent of the iron gates lining St. Charles Avenue, complete with a tented front of the house. As Greg explains, "In New Orleans during Carnival, people have their tents in their front yards. We wanted the energy of the party to start at the gate."

That energy extended into the kitchen where Chefs Mac Edwards, owner of Memphis' Elegant Farmer, and Anthony, Gail and John Uglesich of the eponymous, legendary New Orleans eatery, prepared a brunch fit for a Carnival king or queen. Spirits in the kitchen were high but also strikingly calm. While Mac provided an endless stream of jokes, he and Chef de Cuisine Gannon Hamilton possessed the measured assurance of serious chefs at work. While all seemed calm to the outside observer, Mac explains the inner workings of a restaurant kitchen, "A restaurant is like a duck. The dining room is the top of the duck where everything is calm on the surface of the water. A kitchen is like the legs of the duck when all hell is breaking loose."

The Uglesiches prepared some of their most celebrated dishes, including their signature Shrimp Uggie, with an expertise that one would expect from restaurateurs who managed to serve 400 people in a day while serving only one meal — lunch. As Greg explains the partnership for the afternoon, "It was based on our affinity for the city of New Orleans and pairing the Uglesiches, who are great New Orleans chefs, with a great Memphis chef."

While the chefs fried green tomatoes and boiled brown sugar, guests began the afternoon with mimosas and Gail's famous Bloody Marys in the Heros' New Orleans-style courtyard. Like many guests of Be Nice or Leave, Lucia and Ricky have a long history with New Orleans and own a second home there. "Ricky and I both graduated from Tulane. That's where we met and fell in love. It's a city that we enjoyed so much when we were younger, and we continue to go back because we feel light and happy every time we go."

MAC EDWARDS

MAC EDWARDS has more than 35 years experience in the restaurant industry. He owned and operated McEwen's on Monroe for more than 10 years and was the 2004 Memphis Restaurant Association "Restaurateurs of the Year." In 2011 he opened The Elegant Farmer, which focuses on "elevated" comfort food using the freshest local and regional ingredients from sustainable farms. He is also a founding board member of the Memphis Farmer's Market.

ANTHONY, JOHN AND GAIL UGLESICH

ANTHONY UGLESICH has been in the restaurant industry for over 50 years, after taking over the eponymous legendary New Orleans restaurant from his family. Gail joined him in the business after they married. Uglesich's has been featured in *USA TODAY, National Geographic Traveler Magazine, Food & Wine Magazine* and *The Times-Picayune*, among other publications. Since retiring from the restaurant business in 2005, Anthony, Gail and their son John have established a private catering business and published two cookbooks, *Uglesich's Restaurant Cookbook* and *Cooking with the Uglesiches*.

Serving up memories in Memphis: John, Anthony and Gail Uglesich.

Mac Edwards, owner and chef of the The Elegant Farmer.

"A restaurant is like a duck. The dining room is the top of the duck where everything is calm on the surface of the water. A kitchen is like the legs of the duck when all hell is breaking loose."
–Mac Edwards

'Be Nice or Leave' takes its inspiration from New Orleans folk artist Dr. Bob. As Greg Baudoin explains, "Dr. Bob started painting 'Be Nice or Leave' signs all over the city of New Orleans. It was just a part of New Orleans that we wanted at this party."

Greg Baudoin's Memphis bow to New Orleans' Mardi Gras beads.

As longtime veterans of the New Orleans restaurant scene, the Uglesiches greeted many guests who have fond memories of their restaurant. Founded in 1924 by Anthony's father, Uglesich's had been a seafood institution at its original location on Baronne Street. Recounting the evolution of Uglesich's, Anthony says, "It was a typical New Orleans poboy and seafood place in the beginning, and everything was fried. But over the years we changed our menu as people started to watch what they ate." After Anthony took over the business, Gail gradually became his partner. "It was a mom and pop operation," she recalls. "We were responsible for every aspect of it including all of the sauces, and we were very particular."

On May 7, 2005, the Uglesiches retired from the business and closed their restaurant. They still own the property, and plan to renovate it and give it its rightful place as a historic landmark. After Hurricane Katrina, in August 2005, the Uglesiches moved to Memphis. Though they consider themselves "retired," the Uglesich family has not slowed down. They have taken their food from the restaurant to private catering. Today John is learning all of the tricks of the trade. He organizes all of their engagements and has published a cookbook of his family's recipes, *Cooking with the Uglesiches*. Their legacy has not gone unnoticed in New Orleans or Memphis. "It was great to have them be a part of our event," says Lucia. "They are legends, and we were lucky to find out that they were here in Memphis. Their joy for what they do is palpable to everyone present. They relish their total existence in the realm of cooking, serving and making people happy with their food."

Under a most appropriate setting of Mardi Gras bead-covered oaks, guests were treated to a fabulous New Orleans-meets-Memphis brunch. The table settings were a true highlight of the afternoon. The flower arrangements were done by the Garden District, the Memphis floral shop whose name is a nod to the stately New Orleans neighborhood. "I wanted to do a totally modern take on this type of entertaining, drawing from my many New Orleans Mardi Gras experiences," says Greg, recounting his inspiration. "After Mardi Gras, all of the trees are covered in beads that linger long after the passing parade."

A true New Orleans brunch would not be complete without a jazz ensemble, and the Jeremy Schrader Quartet provided the ideal accompaniment for the party. Guests were also treated to a surprise fashion interlude when whimsical headdresses for the ladies and quirky boutonnieres for the men were doled out. These accoutrements were provided courtesy of Mary Seay Taylor, luncheon guest and co-creator of Memphis based Brave Design. Dessert and coffee were served on perfectly mismatched cups and saucers, all handpicked by Lucia at various estate sales.

After the meal, the chefs received an enthusiastic ovation and engaged in a question and answer session from guests eager to talk about Memphis and New Orleans food. The chefs were inextricably linked by their mutual passion for fresh, local food. As lifelong New Orleanians, fresh, local seafood has always been a priority for the Uglesiches. "Anthony was always successful in business," Gail recounts, "because he dealt with fresh Louisiana seafood and that makes a difference." Of his decision to buy local rather than imported seafood, Anthony explains, "I was one of the few people who bought direct. It came from the boat to me. Most people in the restaurant industry today are so cost conscious that they buy import. If you buy import, you don't know how old it is or how safe the water is. The fresher something is, the better it's going to be." As the chef and owner of The Elegant Farmer and a fixture at the Memphis Farmer's Market, Mac has been a tireless promoter of local food. After the meal, he sang the praises of Earl's Catfish in Dundee, Mississippi, owned by Earl and Jill Lake, calling it "another kind of catfish." He urged guests to support their local purveyors, and lamented the fact that "cheap catfish has killed the high-end American catfish market."

After what can only be described as a marathon brunch, guests put on their walking shoes in preparation for the second line. A uniquely New Orleans tradition that has no equivalent in other cities, the second line is a walking celebratory brass band parade that is not about being sad, but getting happy — a costumed parade without a permit. The jazz quartet transformed into the Mighty Souls Brass Band for the event, and revelers followed them down the street waving umbrellas, handkerchiefs and other throws. While it may not have been a typical happening in the neighborhood, and whether it was the food, cocktails, music or perfect weather, Be Nice or Leave guests were certainly inspired to march down the street with abandon. By the end of the afternoon, it was clear that this soiree reflected Lucia and Ricky's desire to create an event with a New Orleans ambiance, calling forth the feeling that everyone is welcome and *laissez les bons temps rouler.*

The vintage French lace tablecloth purchased by Greg Baudoin in Paris.

Perfectly mismatched plates paired with Alexa Pulitzer of New Orleans place cards.

A little taste of everything, including mimosas and opera was served in the courtyard. Opera Memphis provided the pre-brunch entertainment, featuring a treat of a performance by soprano Amanda Boyd, who had exactly six beats to separate four eggs. In a delicious marriage of the culinary and performing arts, she performed "Bon Appétit!", a one-woman short opera about Julia Child baking a French chocolate cake. This musical piece was a big hit at the inaugural Midtown Opera Festival.

Amanda Boyd

Michael Preacely, Baritone

The Uglesiches relish in making people happy with their food.

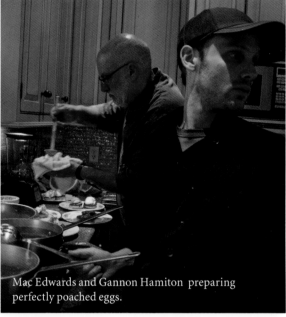

Mac Edwards and Gannon Hamiton preparing perfectly poached eggs.

Chef Mac Edwards and server, Ashley Stem Powell composing the beautiful and refreshing watermelon salad.

Let the festivities begin. L to r: Margaret Ledbetter, formerly of New Orleans, her husband Pierce Ledbetter and Greg Campbell.

Raising their glasses to merriment and Mardi Gras. Ken Hall, Lee Plesofsky, Juli Eck, Damon Arney, Susan Arney, Robin Smithwick

L to r: Lucia Heros, Adam Taylor and Ricky Heros

Jeremy Shrader Quartet. L to r: Art Edmaiston, Sean Murphy, John Bass

The chefs take their bows and answer questions from attentive guests.

The lanterns hanging from the tent, an ode to the lanterns lining St. Charles Avenue.

Lucia Heros, Margaret Ledbetter and Mary Seay Taylor, fashionably adorned from head...

...to toe.

Jonny Ballinger (middle) with his mother Rosemary and father Lynn.

Richard Frymire, Michelle Frymire

L to r: Mary Seay Taylor, Greg Baudoin, Lucia Heros

Served from Epiphany to Fat Tuesday, the King Cake is a centuries old French tradition. Representing baby Jesus, the plastic King Cake baby is hidden inside the doughy, sugary round cake and whoever takes that piece must keep Carnival season going and buy the next cake.

Greg Campbell gets to bring the next cake.

Ann Smithwick shows off Brave Designs headdress, the ultimate lagniappe.

Jennifer McCullogh, also known as Chef Jenn, owner of Chef Jenn Frozen Foods.

Lucia Heros

Mike Mullis in a sea of fine feathered friends. Left: Leslie, his wife.

Michelle Frymire

Zulu Social Club throw, quite a catch.

Muses Krewe shoes.

Lauren Boyer collects beads for the second liners.

Second liners living it up on Lombardy.

Susan Schadt

L to r: Pierce Ledbetter and Greg Baudoin

Mighty Souls Brass Band leads the procession.

L to r: Ken Hall, Mona Sappenfield, Bill Sappenfield

L to r: Robin Smithwick, Juli Eck, Lee Plesofsky, Ann Smithwick

SHRIMP UGGIE

GAIL, ANTHONY AND JOHN UGLESICH

NOTE:
Leave the tail on the shrimp, it helps prevent shrinkage.

- 3 CUPS VEGETABLE OIL
- 1 CUP KETCHUP
- ½ (5 OUNCE) BOTTLE MELINDA EXTRA HOT SAUCE
- 2 TABLESPOONS FRESH LEMON JUICE
- 2 TABLESPOONS SALT
- 2 TEASPOONS FINELY CHOPPED FRESH PARSLEY
- 2 TEASPOONS PAPRIKA
- 4 TEASPOONS CRUSHED RED PEPPER
- 1 SMALL PURPLE ONION, COARSELY CHOPPED
- 1 GREEN BELL PEPPER, COARSELY CHOPPED
- 4 SMALL TO MEDIUM RED OR YUKON GOLD POTATOES
- 16 TO 20 MEDIUM SHRIMP, PEELED AND DEVEINED, WITH TAILS ON

Mix all ingredients, except shrimp and potatoes, in a container and marinate in the refrigerator overnight.

Boil potatoes and cut into 1-inch cubes.

Remove sauce from refrigerator and stir well. Place shrimp and potatoes in a skillet. Using a ladle, dip into bottom of sauce and pour over shrimp and potatoes. Sauce should partly cover ingredients in skillet. Reserve any leftover sauce for another use.

Cook over medium heat, stirring constantly, until shrimp turn pink or to desired degree of doneness.

Divide ingredients between 2 plates and sprinkle with chopped parsley.

Makes 2 generous entrée servings.

GAIL'S FAMOUS BLOODY MARY

GAIL, ANTHONY AND JOHN UGLESICH

- ICE CUBES
- 1 (12 OUNCE) GLASS
- ¼ TEASPOON HORSERADISH
- WORCESTERSHIRE SAUCE
- CELERY SALT
- BLACK PEPPER
- ⅙ PIECE OF LIME
- 3½ OUNCE PREMIUM VODKA
- RED EYE HABANERO
- PICKLED OKRA

Place ice cubes in the glass.

Add horseradish.

Drizzle Worcestershire sauce over the ice cubes.

Sprinkle celery salt over the ice.

Sprinkle a little black pepper.

Squeeze lime in the glass.

Fill the glass half way with premium vodka.

Fill the other half of the glass with Red Eye Habanero.

Stir well and place pickled okra on top.

FRIED GREEN TOMATOES WITH BOILED SHRIMP AND GAIL'S RÉMOUALDE SAUCE

GAIL, ANTHONY AND JOHN UGLESICH

- CANOLA CORN OIL
- EGG BEATER
- 1 GREEN TOMATO, SLICED ¼ INCH THICK
- PLAIN FINE BREAD CRUMBS
- BOILED SHRIMP
- GAIL'S RÉMOULADE SAUCE

Pour oil into a deep frying pot and heat to 350 degrees.

Pour egg beater into a bowl.

Dip sliced green tomatoes into egg beater and lightly coat with bread crumbs.

To test if the oil is hot enough, throw a pinch of the bread crumbs into the oil; if it bubbles to the top, then it is ready to fry.

Place tomatoes into the fryer and cook on one side for 1 minute.

Flip tomatoes to cook on the reverse side for 1 minute.

Remove tomatoes and drain on paper towels.

Top with boiled shrimp and Gail's Rémoualde Sauce, available at uglesichs.com.

WATERMELON SALAD WITH MUSCADINE VINAIGRETTE

MAC EDWARDS

MUSCADINE VINAIGRETTE:

- ¾ CUP MUSCADINE JUICE
- ¼ CUP CIDER VINEGAR
- ¼ CUP HONEY
- 1 CUP OLIVE OIL
- 1 PINCH SALT

Blend juice, vinegar and honey in a food processor.

Process and slowly add olive oil.

Add salt.

SALAD:

- ½ POUND ARUGULA LEAVES
- 1 WATERMELON, CUT INTO 1½ INCH CHUNKS
- ½ POUND FETA CHEESE

Toss arugula with desired amount of vinaigrette.

Top the salad with watermelon and feta or toss it in with the salad.

CATFISH BENEDICT WITH HOLLANDAISE SAUCE

MAC EDWARDS

HOLLANDAISE SAUCE:

- 2 STICKS UNSALTED BUTTER
- 3 SMOKED AND DRIED MARCONI PEPPERS OR SMOKED AND DRIED SWEET PEPPER OF YOUR CHOICE
- WATER
- 3 EGG YOLKS
- ¼ CUP LEMON JUICE
- DASH OF CAYENNE
- PINCH OF SALT, TO TASTE

POACHED EGGS:

- WATER, TO FILL POT
- ½ CUP WHITE VINEGAR
- 4 EGGS

ASSEMBLY:

- TOASTED ENGLISH MUFFINS
- TOMATOES, SLICED
- SMOKED CATFISH FILLETS, CUT IN HALF
- POACHED EGGS
- HOLLANDAISE SAUCE

Melt butter in a saucepan over low heat.

In a separate saucepan, cook peppers with water to cover over low heat until rehydrated, adding water as necessary. Once peppers are rehydrated, drain and puree them in a food processor. Set aside.

Put egg yolks in the top bowl of a double boiler over low heat. Add lemon juice to egg yolks. Stir constantly until eggs start to cook turning pale and thickening. Once eggs turn pale, slowly ladle melted butter while stirring eggs vigorously. Add cayenne and salt to taste. Add half of rehydrated peppers or to taste.

TO POACH EGGS:

Fill a large saucepan ¾ full with water and add white vinegar. Bring to a simmer over medium heat. While gently stirring water, add 4 eggs, one at a time, and continue to gently stir for about 45 seconds to 1 minute. Remove eggs with a slotted spoon and immediately assemble recipe.

TO ASSEMBLE:

Place English muffin on a plate. Top with a tomato slice, half of a fish fillet and a poached egg; pour Hollandaise Sauce over top. Serves 4

"The English muffins are made by Sheri McElvie. She bakes out of her house. It's like English muffins to the tenth power. I like to put them on a flat grill or in a skillet and put a little weight on them so you can get that crust on them. That's what makes them good." –Mac Edwards

GIBSON'S DONUT BREAD PUDDING WITH CARAMEL SAUCE

MAC EDWARDS

- 1 DOZEN DAY OLD DONUTS
- 1 CUP HEAVY CREAM
- 1 CUP MILK
- ½ CUP SUGAR
- 5 EGGS

Cut each donut into 8-10 pieces.

Bring heavy cream, milk and sugar to a boil in a saucepan. In a separate bowl, beat eggs. Temper eggs with hot cream mixture one ounce at a time.

Once the custard is made, pour it over the donuts in a baking pan, covering them about halfway. Press donuts down so they soak up custard. Let pan sit for 15 minutes before baking.

Cover pan with aluminum foil and bake at 350 degrees for 30 minutes and bake another 15 minutes if necessary.

FOR THE CARAMEL SAUCE:

- ¼ CUP WATER
- 1 CUP BROWN SUGAR
- 2 TABLESPOONS BUTTER
- ¼ CUP HEAVY CREAM

Add just enough water (about ¼ cup) to brown sugar in a saucepan so that it starts to liquefy when you heat it.

Bring water and sugar to a boil. Add butter, stirring in until it boils. Add heavy cream and bring to a boil.

Serve bread pudding with caramel sauce and dust with powdered sugar or whipped cream.

Guests left with the ultimate party favors: a cookbook and coffee.

Hosts, Ricky and Lucia Heros

A three-generation family business, Cafe Las Flores is run by Lucia and her siblings. Cafe Las Flores is Nicaragua's finest coffee company committed to sustainable farming practices and social responsibility in surrounding communities.

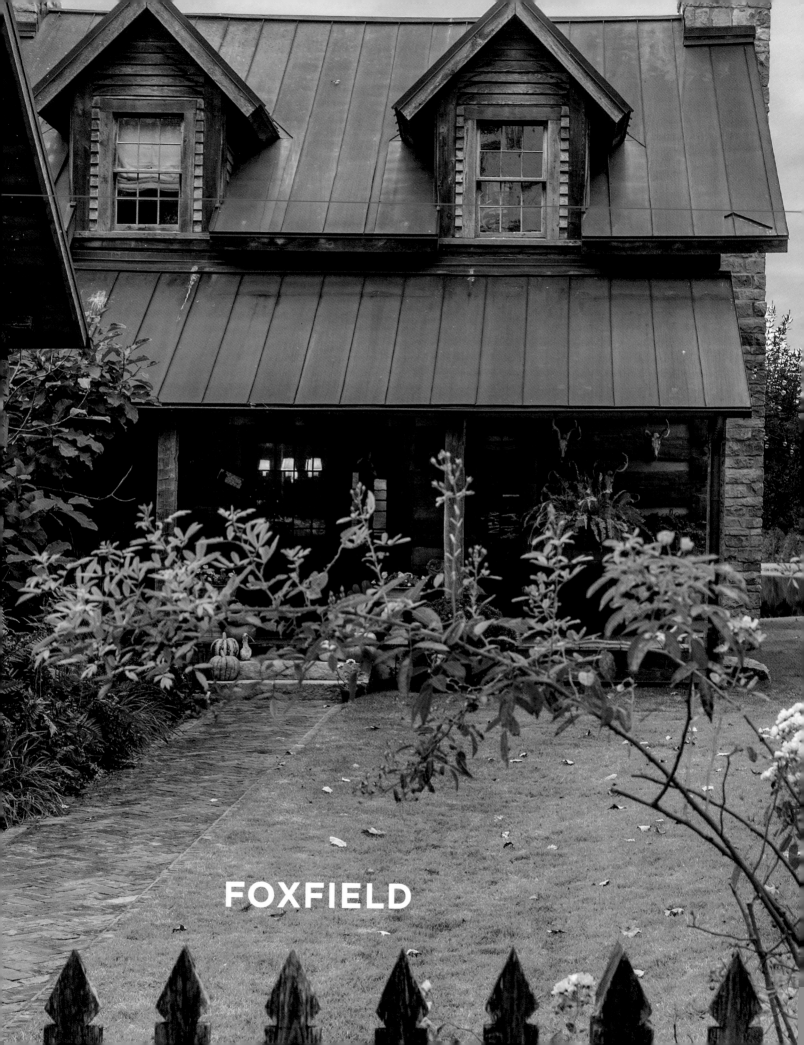

FOXFIELD

AT ITS BEST, A PARTY CAN TRANSCEND THE CATEGORY OF "EVENT" AND TRULY CALL ITSELF A CELEBRATION. The three-day, three-part Culinary Series undertaking hosted by Michelle and Bill Dunavant at their farm, Foxfield, accomplished this transcendence. It was not simply a series of events but truly a celebration of the arts, good food, the out-of-doors, community, teamwork, and talent in many forms. From cocktails and fireworks on Friday night, to a five-course dinner and a performance by Valerie June on Saturday, to grits, grillades and woodturning on Sunday afternoon, this trio of parties combined to create an unforgettable weekend of fun and fellowship for hosts, guests, chefs and stylists.

FOXFIELD FRIDAY COCKTAILS

While Foxfield is tucked away not far outside the city limits of Memphis, as you travel down its gravel road you feel as though you are being transported to tranquil woodlands in a remote corner of the world. Foxfield is the result of over two decades of work and devotion, and it represents an escape for Michelle and Bill Dunavant. It allows them to slow down and spend time with their family and friends in the out-of-doors. It is also a place that they generously share with others, hosting gatherings ranging from family weddings to fundraising events like ArtsMemphis' Culinary Series.

The property includes two lakes, wooded acreage and a bounty of natural resources. The area's natural beauty is highlighted by the perfectly situated and appointed cabin that allows guests to sit a spell, cook a meal or stay the night. The cabin was constructed by using segments of original nineteenth century structures, including Bill's grandparents' smokehouse, and it is beautiful on the inside and the outside. Eighteenth century wooden beams salvaged from a historical site in Maryland give the cabin its historic, rustic feel. Comfortable sofas and a lovely kitchen update the cabin with modern practicalities, and a generously sized screened back porch provides a perfect spot to take in the beauty of the land. "The development of Foxfield took a long time and a lot of hard work," says Bill. "It did not happen overnight."

This spirit of hard work and dedication to nature and the out-of-doors influenced the chefs' vision for the weekend. Miles McMath, Director of Culinary Operations at St. Jude Children's Research Hospital, led the charge, along with a large team of chefs, all vital to the weekend's success: Rick Farmer, St. Jude executive chef, Kevin Shockency, executive chef of the Memphis Hunt and Polo Club, and Lee Richardson from Little Rock. As a chef who ensures that multitudes are fed each day and accommodates palates from around the world with numerous dietary restrictions, Miles was the perfect candidate to be the mastermind behind a weekend that required expert planning and execution, but also flexibility and accommodation.

Local food was central to the weekend's menus. Miles grew up hunting and fishing and learned the essentials of the South's rich culinary traditions at an early age. He was born and raised in rural Alabama and experienced his family growing, raising and gathering their own food. This set the stage for his career as a chef, and his commitment to serving local and seasonal fare. "I have always wanted to do a three-day fire and bring together a group of chefs and artisans for a camp-type experience in a secluded area," he says. "We would build a fire, and cook three or four days' meals off that fire. The idea was for people to camp three days and no one would leave during that time. They would have breakfast, lunch and dinner each day, and then write a story about it. To make it work for ArtsMemphis, we changed it up but we still had the communal lighting of the fire, the dinner and

RICK FARMER

RICK FARMER is the Executive Chef at St. Jude Children's Research Hospital. He has been in the foodservice industry for over forty years. He worked in Memphis, Nashville, San Francisco and New York before continuing his studies in France and other European countries. In 1994 Rick opened Jarrett's Restaurant before teaching at L'École Culinaire until 2012, when he joined St. Jude.

MILES McMATH

MILES McMATH is the Director of Culinary Operations at St. Jude Children's Research Hospital. A lifelong hunter and fisherman, Miles is passionate about using local, organic and humanely grown produce, livestock and game in his cooking. He maintains the garden at St. Jude. Chef McMath has been the owner of three successful restaurants and has recorded over 100 cooking segments for local television show *Mid South Living*, where he appeared weekly for four years. He also appeared on the Food Network's *Simon Super Chefs Live* and is a five-time Gold Medal winner in National American Culinary Federation (ACF) competitions.

LEE RICHARDSON

The New Orleans restaurant scene provided LEE RICHARDSON with opportunities to work with and learn from top-notch chefs, including Kevin Graham, Emeril Lagasse and John Besh. Rising to the rank of chef de cuisine at Besh's celebrated Restaurant August, Richardson was led, in the aftermath of Hurricane Katrina, to Little Rock. The former chef of Ashley's at The Capital Hotel and The Packet House in Little Rock, he leads an ambitious culinary tour de force focused on defining Arkansas' place in Southern food. He has been a three-time semifinalist nominee for the James Beard Best Chef: South, and has been featured in several national magazines, including *Food Arts*, *Garden & Gun*, *Bon Appétit* and *Gourmet*.

KEVIN SHOCKENCY

KEVIN SHOCKENCY has been Executive Chef of the Memphis Hunt and Polo Club since 1998. Kevin grew up in Marion County, Kentucky, in a family that fished, hunted, raised cattle, grew their own vegetables and made their own butter. That dependence on locally raised, fresh food has influenced his cooking style ever since. A graduate of the Culinary Institute of America, Kevin has been a chef at several private clubs, including Eagles Landing Country Club in Stockbridge, Georgia; Jennings Mill Country Club in Athens, Georgia; and Jackson Country Club in Jackson, Tennessee.

then the brunch. The plan was meant to bring chefs and food people together and have them work together."

The chefs worked together in perfect harmony, and all spoke highly of each other professionally and personally. Kevin was eager to join this project. "I was all in because Miles is such a brilliant mind. He thinks outside the box and he loves the out-of-doors. He knows what to do with wild game and wild animals. Whatever his thought process was, I bought into it instantly because it was Miles. I've eaten his food for fifteen years now, and I love his work. Miles is at the top of my list to work with."

A weekend with such large ambitions required weeks of planning in order to acquire the necessary animals and produce. Some of the food came from Miles' personal farm and garden. The chefs also worked closely with the Dunavants in preparation for the event. Michelle and Bill went above and beyond their duties as hosts, opening up Foxfield to the chefs months before the event, and pitching in their own wild game and produce from Michelle's garden. As Miles recounts, the event was truly communal, "The most important thing to me was how the animals were raised and butchered," he says. "Then these guys came in and turned it into all this magnificent stuff. All of the ingredients were in our backyards. Bill Dunavant killed two deer. All of the bass came out of his pond, and the dove was from his friends. There wasn't any money that went into this thing. We went and dug up pieces of steel lying around his place to build fire grates."

The chefs were entering uncharted territory in terms of cooking techniques and surroundings, especially for an event of this magnitude. Inspired in part by Francis Mallmann's cookbook, *Seven Fires: Grilling the Argentine Way* and the Patagonian tradition of whole-animal cooking called *asado*, the fire pit was the central feature of cooking, and it presented a series of challenges for even these seasoned chefs. As Lee explains, "Working on the grill is a slower pace. You can't hurry it up. You can't make things happen until they're ready. It's a different approach to cooking. When you have a 48-hour bonfire, making an adjustment to what you're cooking is like turning a battleship. It's a slow curve to get things changed. You can burn the meat or serve it raw, so that can make for an unsettling approach."

Rick Farmer echoes this sentiment, "When you're going into an event like that, there's a lot of uncertainty. None of us had done that style of cooking before. It's a situation where you get there and get set up, and that's when you get inspired. That's when your gears start turning, and then you really realize what's going on." While the chefs originally planned to create a menu for the weekend, they realized that would not work with this style of cooking. As Miles remembers, "We got a little frustrated because we had farmers dropping things off for us, and we wanted everything to be as local as possible. We didn't really know what we were going to have ahead of time. So then we decided to just start talking about cooking techniques. Let's just recreate a kitchen out there and take our animals and just go cook."

As the chefs soldiered on through the weekend, "Let's just go cook," became a mantra and rallying cry that ultimately led them to victory. They provided guests with an unforgettable experience, starting when they arrived on Friday night for a cocktail party like no other. The night was beautiful when guests arrived, and they were greeted by the stunning natural sight of the lake surrounded by a dramatic, colorful tree line.

Stylists for the event were Erick New, co-owner of Garden District, and Mimsie Crump, co-chair of the 2013 Culinary Series. Their vision for the weekend's decor enhanced Foxfield's natural beauty and ensured that all elements of the weekend came together for guests. "It was such a beautiful canvas, so we didn't want to put anything in there that didn't make sense," says Mimsie. "The food concept was so integral to the whole party, and we wanted the guests to be able to enjoy that aspect of the evening and see the beauty in it."

The stylists organized the weekend around two large central structures: the arbor in front of the lake and the fire pit for the chefs. As Mimsie recalls, "We needed a central structure to ground the space, one that we could decorate in different ways, and that could be used throughout the entire weekend. That's when the idea of the arbor came up." Erick explains, "We made the arbor the center for gathering, and then there was the fire and the cooking area. The tables that Bill had made could be used for serving and that enabled the guests to interact with the chefs. Because it's a farm and it's all out-of-doors, we wanted the decor to be as simple as possible but still look different everyday."

Guests enjoyed portions of grilled meat, prepared salads, charcuterie, cheesy potato chips and bread, and no one left hungry. The accessible and well-lit fire pit allowed guests to interact with the chefs, and learn where the food came from and how it was prepared. In addition to being well fed, guests were also well served with mojitos as the signature drink along with a host of other available libations.

Entertainment for the evening came from The Memphis Dawls, a local favorite whose funky, folksy tunes and signature style recall a past era with a modern twist. Though they began playing together in high school, the Dawls went their separate ways geographically before returning to Memphis and reuniting their group. Today they tour regionally but play many shows in Memphis. Each event during the weekend included a participating RiverArtsFest artisan. Glassblower Teresa White began the weekend by demonstrating her technique and showing off her wares.

The evening concluded with a bang as fireworks lit up the night sky. The show consisted of several minutes of large, brilliantly colored bursts before the true lighting of the bonfire. The finale was a ground shaking explosion that set the ceremonial pile on fire and served as a reminder that fire was the central feature of the weekend.

Michelle and Bill Dunavant opened up Foxfield to the chefs months before the event, and pitched in their own wild game and produce from Michelle's garden. L to r: Harry Dunavant, Bill Dunavant, Billy Dunavant, Michelle Dunavant, Chef Rick Farmer

Bill Dunavant begins staging the fire pit, the focal point of the entire weekend.

The perfectly built bonfire, showstopper of the night, served as a reminder that fire was the central feature of the weekend.

FROM THE FIRE

'Honey Bear', Butternut, Spaghetti & Acorn Squash
Scarlett Queen Turnips, 'Black Beauty' & Japanese Eggplant
'Red Choi' & Dwarf Green Pac Choi, Hon Tsai Tai,
'Bright Lights' Rainbow Chard, **Woodson Ridge Farm**

Satsumas, **Belle Chase, LA**

AR Black & Mutzu Apples, **South AL**

Fingerling Sweet Potatoes & Snap Beans, **Vardaman, MS**

Mustard & Collard Greens, **Po Boy Farms**

Kent Walker Cheese, **Little Rock**

WHOLE ANIMAL COOKERY

Baron of Beef, **Claybrook Farms**

Berkshire Pigs, **Newman Farms**

Tennessee Meat Goats, **Po Boy Farms**

Kent Walker Cheese, **Little Rock**

This menu is free of pesticides, synthetic fertilizers, insecticides, antibiotics, hormones, is GMO-free, and naturally and humanely sourced from regional farmers and fair trade cooperatives, celebrating community and **REAL FOOD.**

ACCOUTREMENTS

Chimichurris   Horseradish Aïoli
Tapenades   Salsa Criolla   Salsa Lucia
Gremolata   Pan Jus

HORNO DE BARRO

Pan de Campo
Fry Bread
Chapa
Cremona

Chef Miles' son, Grant is known as the chicken whisperer.

Second stage of the fire pit where a cord and a half of hickory and oak were used through the weekend.

Lake to table, Bill Dunavant

Stylist, Erick New co owner of the Garden District.

Chef Miles McMath and team. Everyone smelled like smoke for several days, not battle wounds but battle smells.

The Patagonian tradition of whole animal cooking called *asado*, ...
Johnny Siv, Catering Manager at St. Jude Children's Research Hospital

Erick New

Stylist, Mimsie Crump, Co-Chair of the Culinary Series

Chef Rick Farmer, known to be a master with sausage and the charcuterie.

Steamship round of beef.

Instead of chafing dishes, the cooks put stones into the fire and then onto the plate where they would sizzle and smoke to keep the meat warm.

An artist representative from the RiverArtsFest. Glassblower, Teresa White.

Chef Miles McMath opens the door to the Friday night Menu.
The venison, doves and bass were all from Foxfield.

Doors and barrels played a key role, nobs and all.

"We needed a central structure to ground the space that we could decorate in different ways and be up there for the whole weekend. It was such a beautiful canvas, we didn't want to put something there that didn't make sense." –Stylist, Mimsie Crump

Email from Bill Dunavant to chefs, "It's dove season, should I stock up for you?"

L to r: Chef Kevin Shockency gets help from L'École Culinaire student, Uday Purohit.

For a more rustic look, Bill Dunavant had the idea of flipping the tables to use their underside.

Chef Lee Richardson

Guests enjoy the game.

Chef Miles McMath serves up host, Bill Dunavant. Miles says, "Bill is the best guy to work with."

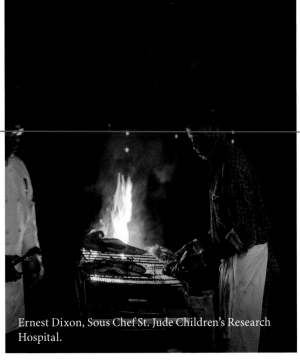

Ernest Dixon, Sous Chef St. Jude Children's Research Hospital.

Guest Cindy Weatherly, the guests and the table aglow.

"It was menu prohibitive. You just had to roll with the punches. It's cooking until the log rolls or the wind changes. There's a million and one variables. It's the ultimate camping trick. Chuck wagon 5400." –Chef Michael Vetro, Catering Manager at St. Jude.

"Ernest Dixon was walking around answering questions and tending to that fire as if he were working there for his lifetime. When I learned that he had worked a whole day at the hospital and arrived a few hours before, it was very profound."
–Chef Lee Richardson

L'École Culinaire student, Monique, Gretchen McLennon

L to r: Bill Sappenfield and wife Mona, Becca Belz

The Memphis Dawls, Jana Misener, Holly Cole, Krista Wroten

"When you arrive at Foxfield, nature envelops you. We have created a nature canvas for people to come out and paint. You can paint it however you want it. The canvas changes constantly. That's what makes it special and sustainable. This canvas changed three times in three days."
–Bill Dunavant

FOXFIELD SATURDAY DINNER

The fire pit glowed through the night on Friday, long after cocktail party guests left, and gave way to a more intimate dinner on Saturday. Mojitos and spit-roasted pigs were replaced by champagne flutes and a five-course meal served on fine china. And even though Saturday's party did not have the pyrotechnics of Friday, guests were treated to an equally spectacular show when internationally famous songstress Valerie June lit up the night with her matchless talent and charm.

Despite their hard work the night before, the team was back in action before sunrise on Saturday morning, tending to the flames and preparing for the festivities to come. In true pioneer fashion, breakfast consisted of cracklin and bacon cooked in cast iron skillets over an open flame.

With the chefs hard at work on the culinary portion of the party, Mimsie Crump, Erick New and team members from Garden District worked throughout the day to transform the casual cocktail party decor of Friday into a stunning setting for a dinner party for twenty-four guests. One long table under an arbor overlooking the lake was a dramatic statement when it was filled from one end to the other with beautiful fall arrangements in heirloom julep cups.

As Erick explains, "Since this was a seated dinner, we wanted it to be more intimate. So we used Mimsie's silver goblets, julep cups and flatware." Mimsie expounds on the effect, "We used Karlee Hickman of Procellar's mismatched china. For the centerpieces, those were pheasant feathers that I had, and then we used pelts around the base and the bar. We used orchids, eucalyptus, hipericum and brasilia foliage."

Guests for the evening arrived at Foxfield just as the sun was setting. There was a breathtaking display of clouds over the sky as the guests sipped champagne and watched the sun light-up the tree line. In keeping with the rustic, yet sophisticated feel of the night, ladies donned their fur vests and knee-high boots. RiverArtsFest artisan potter Lisa Hudson demonstrated her prowess on the pottery wheel for guests. After a cocktail hour, which was filled with the pleasure of natural beauty, good conversation and a group photo for posterity, the party was seated, grace was said and the wine was poured. Though guests settled in for a long, five-course meal, no one stayed too long in their chairs. Instead, after each course, the ladies switched seats and eventually ended the meal seated beside their husbands. This active style of dining kept conversation fresh and flowing and ensured that many hugs were exchanged as diners moved from one seat to the next.

For the meal, the chefs used the meat cooked on the outdoor fire during the day but moved their operations to the cabin kitchen to finish preparations and serve each course. Though the dinner was a collaboration, Lee Richardson served as the lead on this meal. "I took the role Saturday night of helping the chefs pull things together," he says. "We elected to cook inside to organize the final heating, plate assembly and service." The meal began with a beautiful salad followed by a butternut squash soup. Guests were

blown away by the scaloppini, a perfect autumn dish that was the centerpiece of a perfect autumn meal. The dinner concluded with an oven baked apple tart a la mode topped with a rich caramel sauce.

Michelle recalls her reaction after their first talk with Miles about his ideas for these events: "I thought 'this is never going to happen. The vision he had of the fires and all of the outdoor cooking. I wondered how they would ever put this thing together and thought 'there's no way.' But they did indeed put it together and the results were awesome. All of the food was amazing, from start to finish."

For Lee, the food preparation and the entire weekend at Foxfield represented an important moment in his twenty-year culinary career. "During these years I have been resistant to the idea of 'chef as artist.' In the context of this event, combined with the wide variety of art that we had available to us, it brought this concept together for me. It made me more comfortable in terms with what I do, in my mind and in my heart-of-hearts, as artistry. Also, in my work, I attempt to create an emotional response from the people that we serve, and also one from myself."

Reflected in Lee's sentiment were Bill's remarks made at the dinner table that evening about Foxfield and his philosophy behind it. Always the consummate host, Bill made a series of remarks celebrating the chefs and presented them with gifts from his travels. During his toast, he remarked, "When you arrive at Foxfield nature envelops you. We created a nature canvas for people to come out and paint. You can paint it however you want. We can go for a walk at different times of the year and the canvas changes every time. That's what makes it special and sustainable."

The final stroke of artistry for the evening came with Valerie June's musical performance. The party moved from the dinner table near the lake to a seating area created for the evening in front of the cabin's porch. Guests cozied up on lawn furniture and under vintage quilts to have one more drink or a cup of coffee. The whimsical, retro furniture, provided by Propceller, perfectly complemented Valerie's self-described "organic moonshine roots music."

Originally from Humboldt, Tennessee, Valerie considers Memphis her formative city. She developed as a musician here, playing gigs in restaurants, clubs and bars and starring in Craig Brewer's MTV series, *$5 Cover*, about the Memphis music scene. After achieving local success, Valerie moved to Brooklyn, and in 2011 The Black Keys' Dan Auerbach produced her album *Pushin' Against a Stone* in Nashville. In addition to touring nationally and internationally, she has graced the likes of *The New York Times, The New York Times Magazine*, National Public Radio and *Austin City Limits* with her unique style of music and matchless charm.

Her intimate performance on the front porch of Foxfield's cabin in front of only a few dozen guests was truly one of a kind. Playing her original songs along with gospel and blues classics that inspired her, Valerie amazed guests with her otherworldly sound, storytelling prowess and striking beauty. She had her hair on top of her head, and she wore boots and a turquoise jacket with eye shadow to match. She regaled guests with tales of her upbringing and her love for

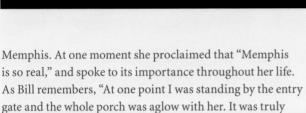

Memphis. At one moment she proclaimed that "Memphis is so real," and spoke to its importance throughout her life. As Bill remembers, "At one point I was standing by the entry gate and the whole porch was aglow with her. It was truly unbelievable."

By the end of the night, all audience members – old fans and those who had never heard her music before – were completely under her spell. For the final number, she invited several guests up to sing with her the classic country folk tune "A Hole in my Bucket" in a rendition that brought back memories of campfire sing-alongs.

Regretfully, the dinner and concert came to a close but guests left Foxfield with full stomachs and rich memories. They also had gained an appreciation for the artistry of the chefs who prepared and served them dinner; had become acquainted with a world-famous musical talent who calls Memphis home; and had enjoyed the natural beauty of Foxfield, which has been fostered over time and was fully on display.

For the final heating and plate assembly and service we took it inside Saturday night.
L to r: L'École Culinaire student, Melvin Davis, Chefs Lee Richardson and Kevin Shockency

While Foxfield is tucked away not far outside the city limits of Memphis, as you travel down its gravel road you feel as though you are being

Chef Lee Richardson gathering greens in Michelle Dunavant's garden.

Stylist, Mimsie Crump and the coveted, customized letterpress lagniappe.

Michael Vetro

Chef Rick Farmer

Chef Johnny Siv from St. Jude Children's Research Hospital.

"Saturday night we did have a menu. That night was special because we had this internationally famous Memphis musician, Valerie June in our midst and she's playing for us."
–Chef Rick Farmer

The cabin was constructed by using segments of original 19th century structures, including Bill's grandparents' smokehouse. Eighteenth century wooden beams salvaged from the nearby countryside give the cabin it's historic, rustic feel:

RiverArtsFest, potter, Lisa Hudson shares her artistry with Kim Labry and husband, Ed.

Bill Dunavant bestowed a chef's perfect bounty. L to r: Michael Vetro, Chef Kevin Shockency, Bill Dunavant, Chefs Lee Richardson, Rick Farmer

"When you have a 48-hour bonfire, making an adjustment to what you are cooking is like turning a battleship."

–Chef Lee Richardson

Ann Leatherman, Chefs Kevin Shockency, Rick Farmer

Stanford Roberts and guest Braxton, John Wilbourn, Jeanne Wilbourn, JoEllyn Slott, Dave Slott, Lewis Williamson, Barbara Williamson, Bobby Leatherman, Ann Leatherman, Bill Dunavant, Michelle Dunavant, Tom Marshall, Lisa Ann Marshall, Ed Labry, Kim Labry, Lisa Putman, Mark Putman, Elizabeth Allen, Bo Allen, Amy Rhodes, Bill Rhodes.

Toasts to the hosts. L to r: Bill Dunavant and wife Michelle

Bill Rhodes and his wife, Amy

L to r: Bill Rhodes, Lewis Williamson, Ed Labry, Bill Dunavant, Dave Slott

"At one point, I was standing by the entry gate and that whole porch was aglow with Valerie June. It was truly unbelievable."

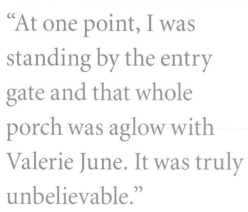

Guests cozied up on lawn furniture and under vintage quilts. The whimsical, retro furniture perfectly complemented Valerie's self-described "organic moonshine roots music."

Playing her original songs along with gospel and blues classics that inspired her, Valerie amazed guests with her otherworldly sound, storytelling prowess and striking beauty.

FOXFIELD SUNDAY BRUNCH

The weekend concluded with a Sunday brunch. The day was sunny and unseasonably warm, providing guests with the perfect setting to be outside and enjoy a delicious meal. The Side Street Steppers provided energetic musical accompaniment for the event and RiverArtsFest artisan Dennis Paullus entranced guests with his wood turning talent.

For the casual but sophisticated brunch, guests sat under the arbor at tables that had been transformed by Mimsie and Erick into daytime decor with flowing pieces of fabric. The tables were decorated with beautiful flower arrangements in antique tea tins from Karlee Hickman's Propcellar collection.

Coffee and mimosas were, of course, on the menu for the morning, in addition to a Bloody Mary bar set up on the multipurpose Propcellar garden stand. Erick emphasized the importance of repurposing different items throughout the weekend to create a different look and feel for each day. "We used what we had in different ways throughout the weekend," he said. Michelle adds, "This spirit of resourcefulness was a reminder of the collaborative nature of the weekend. The chefs came out and saw Mimsie and Erick doing their work and said 'we've got to perform differently for each meal.' The choreography of each event was amazing."

The choreography carried over to the meal itself as chefs moved from the kitchen on Saturday night back to the fire pit on Sunday morning. They used the same ingredients and techniques from throughout the weekend. Brunch was served family style and included a skillet-made hash, greens, and arguably some of the most delicious grits and grillades guests had ever tasted. Lee explains the genesis of that dish, "The red wine brown gravy was a recipe of my grandmother's. I had that up my sleeve for the weekend. She made it with ducks, doves or beef, and I used it for dove breasts for the brunch."

During the brunch, The Side Street Steppers performed their signature, updated Americana folk music to the delighted crowd. A talented foursome, The Side Street Steppers dressed the part for playing funky mountain music and showed off their talents on the banjo, upright bass and washboard.

A main attraction for the afternoon was the work of Dennis Paullus. Guests were in awe of his skill and ability to craft a variety of wooden pieces, including much-coveted muddlers and plates. Since the event, Lee has had him make a few pieces for him.

The end of Sunday brunch marked the end of a long, fruitful weekend of great food, drink and fellowship in the most beautiful of settings. From guests to chefs to hosts, everyone agreed that it was an endeavor that came together because of collaboration and hard work. St. Jude chef Michael Vetro describes the aftermath of the weekend, "Everyone smelled like smoke for several days. We didn't have battle wounds, just battle smells. Everything was collaborative. No one can say 'I made that' because everyone worked on everything together."

And while it required a great deal of time, everyone was happy to contribute. Kevin explains, "I was happy to give up my time because any time you don't have to work in the kitchen and can get outside, that's great. Also the Hunt & Polo Club members are so supportive of having us out and giving back to the community."

Lee, echoing this sentiment, says, "I would do anything I could to free myself up to participate in something like this. One of my own private relishes of doing what I do is that I've had opportunities to experience places like Foxfield. I really love the gathering, the sense of community and enjoyment of all of these spaces that people have created for just that effect. Something that really stayed with me from that weekend was hearing Bill talk about building Foxfield and telling the contractor that the materials and the tools of the craft had to be dated back to another time."

As a host, Bill remarks that Foxfield seems to inspire the sense of camaraderie that made the weekend possible. "That's the way Foxfield is. When we do something there, it's infectious for everyone to pitch in. We cook and we clean up together. It's a place where people want to be involved." And Michelle adds, "We like to do that. Everyone wants to help and to be a part of it."

Brunch was served family style and included some of the most delicious grits and grillades guests have ever tasted. Chef Lee Richardson explains the genesis of that dish, "The red wine brown gravy was a recipe of my grandmother's. I had that up my sleeve for the weekend."

L to r: Julia McDonald, Kathy Gale Uhlhorn

"Chefs are warriors" –Chef Michael Verto L to r: Chefs Lee Richardson, Michael Vetro, Rick Farmer, Kevin Shockency

L'École Culinaire School student, Monique.

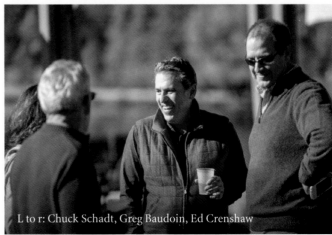
L to r: Chuck Schadt, Greg Baudoin, Ed Crenshaw

Forefront l to r: Gil Uhlhorn, Mike Dragutsky and wife, Beni, Chuck Schadt

The Side Street Steppers performed their signature, updated Americana folk music to the delighted crowd. L to r: Vera Victoria, Christain Stanfield

A relaxing moment for Michelle Dunavant

L to r: Gil Uhlhorn, Mike Dragutsky, Beni Dragutsky, Kathy Gayle Uhlhorn

L to r: Bill Dunavant, Billy Dunavant, Michelle Dunavant

Laura Haralson

The indoor glow,
Michelle Dunavant

A talented foursome, the Side Street Steppers dressed the part for playing funky mountain music and showed off their talents on the banjo, upright bass and washboard.

Rhea Crenshaw

A main attraction for the afternoon was the artistry of Dennis Paullus. Guests were in awe of his skill and ability to craft a variety of wooden pieces, including much-coveted muddlers and plates.

L'École Culinaire students and chefs, Masters at "community" and choreography.

48 HOUR FIRE

- 1 WHOLE PIG MILES' FARM
- 2 DEER FROM FOXFIELD
- RABBITS
- SQUIRRELS
- 250 DOVE
- DUCKS
- RACCOON
- FISH

- AS MANY FISH AS WE CAN CATCH ON THE GROUNDS OF FOXFIELD
- SEVERAL CRATES OF SEASONAL PRODUCE FROM THE AREA
- NUMEROUS ITEMS FORAGED FROM THE GROUNDS OF FOXFIELD
- AN ASSORTMENT OF SHINE AND SPIRITS FROM OUR LOCAL BOOTLEGGERS
- WHATEVER ELSE WE COME UP WITH WITHIN 300 MILE RADIUS
- FIVE ACCOMPLISHED REGIONAL CHEFS:
  - LEE RICHARDSON FORMERLY FROM THE CAPITAL HOTEL IN LITTLE ROCK
  - KEVIN SHOCKENCY FROM THE MEMPHIS HUNT AND POLO CLUB
  - MILES MCMATH, MICHAEL VETRO AND RICK FARMER FROM ST. JUDE CHILDREN'S RESEARCH HOSPITAL
  - L'ÉCOLE CULINAIRE SCHOOL
  - ONE GIFTED BAKER,
  - THREE JACK OF ALL CULINARY TRADES (ERNEST DICKSON, JOHNNY SIV AND PATRICK PRINCE)
  - A ROTATING CREW OF CULINARY AMATEURS, FRIENDS AND NEIGHBORS
- CHERRY, PECAN, HICKORY, OAK LOGS, AND WHATEVER ELSE WE MAY RUN ACROSS ON THE FARM

Build a single wood fire and over the course of 48-plus hours, use it to roast, braise, bake, simmer and grill as many different dishes as possible from within 300 miles — for the ceremonial lighting of the fire cocktail party, the following day's dinner, and the following day's brunch.

BREAKFAST SAUSAGE

MILES McMATH, RICHARD FARMER AND KEVIN SHOCKENCY

SERVINGS: 60

- ⅓ CUP PLUS 1 TABLESPOON PLUS 1 TEASPOON DRIED SAGE
- ⅓ CUP PLUS 1 TABLESPOON PLUS 1 TEASPOON SALT
- 3 TABLESPOONS PLUS 1 TEASPOON GROUND BLACK PEPPER
- 2½ TEASPOONS DRIED MARJORAM
- ½ CUP PLUS 2 TABLESPOONS BROWN SUGAR
- 1¼ TEASPOONS CRUSHED RED PEPPER FLAKES
- 1 TEASPOON GROUND CLOVES
- 20 POUNDS GROUND PORK

In a small bowl, combine the sage, salt, ground black pepper, marjoram, brown sugar, crushed red pepper and cloves. Mix well.

Place the pork in a large bowl and add the mixed spices to it. Mix well with your hands and form into patties.

Sauté the patties in a large skillet over medium high heat for 5 minutes per side, or until internal pork temperature reaches 160 degrees F (73 degrees C).

BRUSSELS SPROUTS WITH BACON

MILES McMATH, RICHARD FARMER AND KEVIN SHOCKENCY

SERVINGS: 12

- ½ POUND SLICED BACON, CHOPPED
- 1 OUNCE EXTRA-VIRGIN OLIVE OIL
- 1 RED ONION, CHOPPED
- 3 POUNDS BRUSSELS SPROUTS, LEFT WHOLE, LARGER SPOUTS HALVED
- ¼ CUP BROWN SUGAR
- SALT AND PEPPER
- 1½ CUPS CHICKEN BROTH
- 2 OUNCES RICH REDUCED BEEF BROTH
- 1½ OUNCES BUTTER

Brown bacon in a medium skillet over medium-high heat. Remove bacon to a paper towel lined plate.

Add extra-virgin olive oil to the pan. Add onions to the pan and sauté 1 to 2 minutes.

Add Brussels sprouts and brown sugar. Season with salt and pepper.

Cook Brussels sprouts 2 to 3 minutes until they begin to soften, and then add stock. Bring to a boil, cover and reduce heat to medium-low. Cook 10 minutes or until almost tender. Add reduced beef stock and cook to form a glaze.

Finish with butter and top with cooked bacon.

CHIMICHURRI

MILES McMATH, RICHARD FARMER AND KEVIN SHOCKENCY

SERVINGS: 2 CUPS

- 3-6 CLOVES OF GARLIC
- 2 TABLESPOONS CHOPPED ONION
- 2 CUPS FRESH PARSLEY AND/OR CILANTRO, FIRMLY PACKED
- ¼ CUP FRESH OREGANO LEAVES (OPTIONAL)
- ½ CUP OLIVE OIL
- 1 TABLESPOON LIME JUICE (OPTIONAL)
- 2 TABLESPOONS RED WINE VINEGAR (OPTIONAL)
- KOSHER SALT AND RED PEPPER FLAKES, TO TASTE

Pulse garlic and onion in a food processor until finely chopped.

Add parsley and/or cilantro, and oregano if using, and pulse briefly, until finely chopped.

Transfer mixture to a separate bowl. Add olive oil, lime juice, and vinegar; stir. (Adding the liquids outside of the blender gives the chimichurri the correct texture. You don't want the herbs to be completely puréed, just finely chopped.)

Season with salt and red pepper flakes to taste.

Store in the refrigerator until ready to serve.

PANZANELLA SALAD WITH FIRE ROASTED WINTER SQUASH AND ROASTED FALL SHALLOT VINAIGRETTE

MILES McMATH, RICHARD FARMER AND KEVIN SHOCKENCY

SERVINGS: 6-8

- 1 (2 POUND) BUTTERNUT SQUASH, SKIN ON, ROASTED IN THE FIRE UNTIL CHARRED
- 14 OUNCES SOURDOUGH BREAD, CUT INTO THICK SLICES, SEASONED WITH OLIVE OIL, GARLIC, SALT AND PEPPER AND GRILLED OVER THE FIRE UNTIL TOASTED
- 8 OUNCES DRIED TART CHERRIES, REHYDRATED IN APPLE JUICE
- 4 OUNCES LOCAL PECANS, TOASTED AND ROUGHLY CHOPPED
- 16 FLUID OUNCES ROASTED SHALLOT VINAIGRETTE, (RECIPE FOLLOWS)
- 1 BUNCH ITALIAN PARSLEY, CHOPPED
- ¼ OUNCES CHIFFONADE FRESH SAGE
- 1 BUNCH SCALLIONS, THINLY SLICED
- SALT AND PEPPER, TO TASTE

Dice roasted squash into 1 inch pieces. Toss squash into a bowl with sliced grilled bread then add rehydrated cherries.

Add Roasted Shallot Vinaigrette, parsley, sage, pecans and scallions; gently fold everything together. Salt and pepper to taste.

Serve at room temperature.

ROASTED FALL SHALLOT VINAIGRETTE

- 4 HEADS GARLIC, SKIN ON, ROASTED IN THE FIRE
- 8 SHALLOTS, SKIN ON, ROASTED IN THE FIRE
- 3 OUNCES BALSAMIC VINEGAR
- 3 OUNCES SHERRY VINEGAR
- 10 OUNCES WALNUT OIL
- 8 OUNCES EXTRA VIRGIN OLIVE OIL
- 2 TEASPOONS CHOPPED FRESH ROSEMARY
- 2 TEASPOONS CHOPPED FRESH THYME
- 1 OUNCE HONEY
- 2 TEASPOONS KOSHER SALT
- 1 TEASPOON FRESHLY GROUND BLACK PEPPER

Squeeze out roasted garlic and shallots into the bowl of a food processor; purée until smooth. Add the vinegars, oils, herbs, honey, salt, and pepper.

DOVES IN RED WINE GRAVY

LEE RICHARDSON, LITTLE ROCK, AR

This recipe is as close to my grandmother Maggie's as I have been able to get in writing. It was, and continues to be, my formal culinary education. It is the combination of the savory experience and celebration of family that took place around her table that inspired me to cook professionally. I don't like to cook the doves as long as I simmer the gravy, but I want the rich flavor of seared proteins to be at the foundation, so, I start the gravy with chicken thighs to accomplish that and to add in a little darkening to the color. In a restaurant setting, I have much better access to dark and rich stocks. When cooking at home, Kitchen Bouquet is the trick I use to be sure the purple color or not so dark brown color gets where I want it to go. Think of the recipe as akin to bore sighting a rifle. It will get you on the target, but you will have to interact with it and adjust it to get it just right. As Janice Joplin famously sang, "You know you got it when it makes you feel good!"

FOR GRAVY (BEST IF PREPARED A DAY IN ADVANCE):

Yield: approximately ½ gallon, serves 6-8

- ¾ cup all-purpose flour + a little for dusting the cheeks
- 2 pounds boneless, skinless chicken thighs
- ½ cup peanut, canola or light olive oil
- 1 cup diced onion
- ½ cup diced celery
- ½ cup diced green pepper
- 3 cloves of garlic, peeled and chopped
- 2 tablespoons tomato paste
- 1 cup red wine
- 3 cups chicken or beef broth
- 4 teaspoons Kitchen Bouquet
- 2 cups water
- 1 teaspoon freshly picked thyme leaves
- 1 tablespoon freshly chopped Italian parsley
- 2 tablespoons Lea & Perrins Worcestershire Sauce
- salt
- pepper

TO FINISH:

- limit of doves (12-16)
- salt and pepper, to taste
- ¼ cup red wine
- 1 gravy recipe

Season and flour chicken thighs. Sear in oil over medium-high heat in a heavy gauge sauté or braising pan. Once browned well, remove the thighs from the pan and add onions, celery, and peppers in succession, allowing the onions to become translucent, before adding the celery and the celery to soften before adding the peppers.

Once the peppers have softened, add garlic followed by tomato paste once the garlic begins to cook. The tomato paste should be allowed to caramelize a little. Add the flour. At this point it is very important to have a wooden spoon. The flour will have to be worked into the mixture and will have to be scraped from the bottom of the pan as it is stirred to prevent burning. Continue to scrape and stir and brown the flour as long as possible until the mixture becomes too dry to work with.

Add wine and continue to stir, taking care to protect the thickening mass from sticking and burning on the bottom of the pan until just about dry.

Add stock and Kitchen Bouquet; thoroughly incorporate while bringing to a boil. Simmer the liquid and reduce to a gravy consistency. Add the chicken thighs back to the pan along with the fresh herbs and seasonings.

Simmer covered on low or in a 275 degree oven for approximately 2 hours. Allow gravy to cool and chill overnight.

Season the doves with salt and pepper. Sear in a cast iron skillet over medium-high heat until they are golden brown on all sides (in batches if needed, removing the seared birds to make room for new ones).

Deglaze with wine, add gravy to the skillet and bring it to a simmer. Add the doves and continue to simmer 15 to 20 minutes.

Serve over creamy grits.

CREAMY STONE GROUND GRITS

LEE RICHARDSON, LITTLE ROCK, AR

THERE IS SOMETHING TRANSCENDENT THAT HAPPENS TO GRITS COOKED WITH A LITTLE BIT OF MILK AND FINISHED WITH MASCARPONE WHEN IT IS AVAILABLE. TOPPED WITH DOVES IN RED WINE GRAVY IT MAKES AN UNFORGETTABLE BRUNCH.

- 3 CUPS WATER
- 1 CUP WHOLE MILK
- ½ TEASPOON SALT
- 1 CUP STONE GROUND GRITS
- 2 TABLESPOONS BUTTER
- 2 TABLESPOONS MASCARPONE (IF UNAVAILABLE, SUBSTITUTE CREAM CHEESE)

In a medium sized, heavy gauge saucepan, over medium heat, bring water, milk and salt to a boil. Slowly whisk in the ground grits and return to a boil. Continue whisking at a boil or near boil until the mixture begins to thicken noticeably.

Reduce the heat to low and continue cooking for another 5 minutes; stirring occasionally. Cover and reduce the heat as low as it will possibly go for another 5 to 10 minutes.

Whisk in butter and mascarpone. Serve immediately with plenty of gravy! Garnish with thinly sliced scallions.

BREAD AND CHOCOLATE

LEE RICHARDSON, LITTLE ROCK, AR

I ABSOLUTELY LOVE THIS NOT-QUITE-A-DESSERT STAND IN FOR DESSERT. IT COULD NOT BE MUCH EASIER NOR MORE PLEASING. INSTANT SMILES, JUST ADD PEOPLE. WHILE PREPARING A WARM CHOCOLATE DIPPING SAUCE FOR DULCE DE LECHE COOKIES, I TOOK ADVANTAGE OF SOME LEFTOVER BREAD FROM THE DINNER SPREAD TO ADD ANOTHER EMBELLISHMENT TO THE DESSERT LINEUP.

- 2 CUPS HEAVY CREAM
- ½ POUND DARK CHOCOLATE
- FRENCH BREAD, SLICED
- WARM CHOCOLATE GANACHE

In a saucepan over medium heat, heat cream until it just begins to rise up the sides of the pan. Be careful, it will boil over aggressively if given a chance. Turn off the heat and pour chocolate into the cream, pushing it around to insure that it is all submerged. Allow to sit for 5 to 10 minutes.

Using a whisk, whip to thoroughly incorporate into a smooth chocolate sauce. If any of the chocolate appears not to have thoroughly melted when you begin whipping, allow it to sit a little longer. Apply a little additional low heat if needed.

Enjoy immediately or hold warm in double boiler, chafing dish or fondue pot. Get it while it's hot!

FUNKYLUX

VISITORS FROM AROUND THE WORLD MAKE
THE PILGRIMAGE to Memphis to stand on some of the
most sacred sites in music history. While Graceland is the
most famous attraction, Memphis boasts an abundance
of places that have been pivotal in our nation's cultural
formation. These include Sun Studios, Beale Street,
Ardent Records and the Stax Museum of American Soul
Music, the only soul music museum in the world. In
the heart of Memphis' Soulsville neighborhood, Stax is
totally unique—no other museum can claim a Soul Train
dance floor or Isaac Hayes' Cadillac. The soulful spot
oozed the juiciness called for in the recipe for FunkyLux,
a high-low soul food revue that celebrated what's best
about Memphis' incomparable music legacy.

Chefs Brown Burch, Jennifer Dickerson and Ben Smith have cooked in a variety of venues, from the finest restaurants across the world to exclusive private homes to their own restaurants in Memphis, but they were all excited by the idea of collaborating in such a unique venue. Jennifer's enthusiasm was palpable. "I was excited because we have all done fine-dining dinner parties for private individuals. But to take it outside and involve Stax made me excited to go outside of the box, but also to elevate the food and highlight the city of Memphis. It all came together to support the arts."

"The parallels between art and music and cuisine are not that far apart. It's something that's really close to all of us. The mental processes involved in music, art and food are very similar." –Ben Smith

As a son, husband and father of artists, Ben also understood the connections between FunkyLux and Memphis' arts community. "Chefs get asked often to participate in fundraisers, and after fifteen years of doing it, it's not about the exposure. It's about the event being something different and that the beneficiary is something that I support. There are parallels between art, music and cuisine; the mental processes involved in the three are very similar."

The creation of the menu for FunkyLux centered around innovative takes on traditional, fresh ingredients and recipes associated with soul food. For Brown, this meant returning to his culinary roots. "My mom's side of the family is from Memphis, and my dad's from Hughes, Arkansas, which is right across the river in the middle of the Delta. They cooked soul food there, so I know soul food. When we were talking about the menu, I was just throwing out soul food ingredients and dishes and ideas and wanted to take those and elevate them."

This idea of elevated soul food manifested itself in everything from dirty rice arancini to deconstructed succotash to frog leg ragout. Guests were treated to a five-course meal, served on fine china by veteran, volunteer servers. The soulful dishes were all accompanied by specialty drinks, including whimsical

BROWN BURCH

BROWN BURCH is a classically trained French chef who has worked for some of the best chefs in the world: David Bouley (Bouley), Charlie Palmer (Aureole), Terrance Brennan (Picholine), and Daniel Boulud (Daniel) — all in New York City. His successful career has led him to the finest kitchens in Palm Beach, Sun Valley, Charleston, New York, Chicago, Florence, and London. During his time abroad he staged at Michelin three-star restaurants, consulted for hotels in the Middle East and Asia, and was opening chef for Le Cirque's location in New Delhi, India. Brown currently is the personal chef for the Hyde family in Memphis.

JENNIFER DICKERSON

JENNIFER DICKERSON has been cooking professionally in Memphis for almost two decades. Her first job was at Cajun Restaurant Cafe Roux making salads and shucking oysters. After some intensive training and on-the-job experience at busy Cooper-Young restaurant Maxwell's, Jennifer rose quickly through the ranks to become Executive Chef at KoTo (where she earned a perfect 4-star rating from *The Commercial Appeal*), McEwen's on Monroe, The Memphis Brooks Museum of Art and Garland's. Then came a six-year stint with a Memphis family as their personal chef, which involved travel and event planning. Back in the restaurant scene since 2012, Jennifer is currently the Executive Chef of Greentree Hunting Club, and owner and Executive Chef of LUXCulinary.com, a Mid-South based personal chef and restaurant consulting business.

BEN SMITH

BEN SMITH is the head chef and owner of Tsunami, Cooper-Young's first fine dining restaurant. A native Memphian, Ben studied at the Culinary Institute of America in Hyde Park, New York, before cooking in San Francisco and at the Lodge at Keole in Lanai, Hawaii. After returning to Memphis he opened Tsunami in July 1998. Ben has been supporting local, sustainable agriculture since 1998, buying from local farmers and hosting a winter farmers' market, in addition to making Tsunami the first Project Greenfork certified restaurant. In 2005 he published the *Tsunami Cookbook*. Ben has been invited to cook at the James Beard House twice, and was named *Restaurateur of the Year* in 2010 by the Memphis Restaurant Association.

Chefs Jennifer Dickerson, Ben Smith and Brown Burch in their appropriately adorned chef jackets, thanks to stylist, Augusta Campbell and her gold glitter stock.

Jennifer Dickerson

Chefs check their version of stock. L to r: Alan Johnson, Ben Smith, Brown Burch

Radiant Holliday Flowers gleam with their back drop, the dinner menu, Stax style, one for the gold record books.

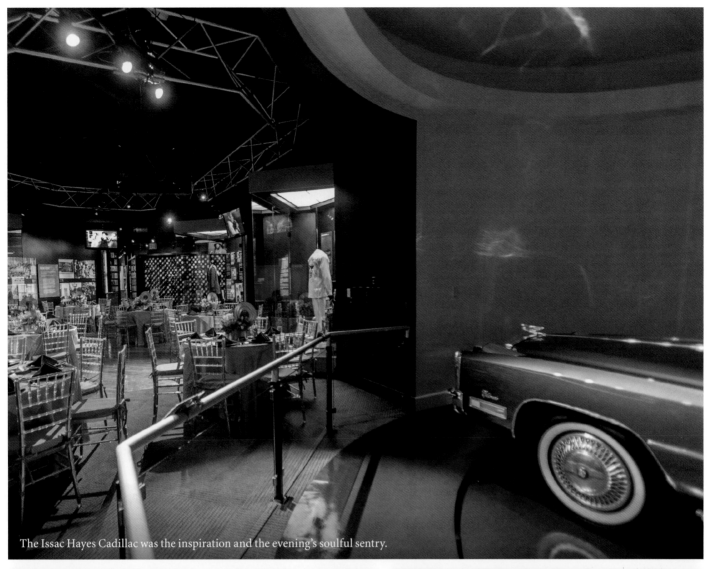

The Issac Hayes Cadillac was the inspiration and the evening's soulful sentry.

Sara Hillyer and Reynolds Hillyer

Allison Galler, Matt Galler

cans of Sofia champagne and an apple moonshine cocktail artfully presented in a highball glass.

Stylist Augusta Campbell ensured the backdrop for this soul food feast was appropriately funky, drawing her inspiration from Isaac Hayes' teal-and-gold-adorned Cadillac that spun slowly on display as guests polished off their meals. She explains that when she started planning the look of the party with the chefs' ideas, "the Cadillac was the inspiration. We thought that tacky-chic with all of the teal and gold would look great and make the evening fun." From the tablecloths and napkins to the plates, Augusta sprinkled the teal-and-gold-color palette throughout. A highlight of the decor included a centerpiece with a gold record menu in homage to Stax. "The gold record is a nod to Stax, all of its hit records and its history. Being in that venue was so fulfilling because it's such a great place."

And as a professional stylist and the fashion editor of *Memphis Magazine*, Augusta also ensured that everyone's fashion was on point. In the mode of a method actor, she adorned 70s styles for weeks before the main event and was on a vintage shopping mission for the perfect find. She wore a vintage Lily Rubin dress that reflected her shining passion and the gold decor. For chefs Jennifer, Brown and Ben, she spray painted black chef jackets with glitter and styled the servers' outfits, providing them with vintage tuxedo shirts inspired by advertisements from the 1970s.

After dinner, legendary Memphis soul band The Bo-Keys gave a performance that got guests onto their feet. Brown reasoned that if FunkyLux was to be a soul food revue, then, naturally, the party needed Southern Soul Music and the iconoclastic Memphis Sound. "The Bo-Keys are the best soul music band in the world. I love Memphis music and soul music, so I gave them a call and sold them on the idea," says Brown. Formed in 1998 by Scott Bomar as a backing band for former Stax artist Sir Mack Rice, The Bo-Keys embody the Memphis sound and are part of the city's long-standing tradition of talented working musicians.

Memphians Jim Stewart and his sister Estelle Axton founded Stax Records in the late 1950's (Stewart took the first two letters from his last name and added the first two letters of his sister's last name to form "Stax"). The label eventually evolved into a true musical and cultural force with a lasting impact on music in Memphis and around the world.

Stax's story mirrors Memphis' rise and fall as a national leader in the music recording industry, launching the careers of unknowns such as Isaac Hayes, Otis Redding, the Staple Singers, Wilson Pickett, Luther Ingram, Albert King, The Bar-Kays, Booker T. & the M.G.'s, Johnnie Taylor, Rufus and Carla Thomas, along with dozens of other artists, including legendary songwriter, David Porter.

After enjoying decades of success and hits, Stax Records closed its doors in 1975, and its building eventually fell into disrepair and was demolished in 1989. Thanks to a group of dedicated philanthropists and civic leaders who created the Soulsville Foundation in 1998, the dilapidated recording studio was returned to its former glory. In addition to creating a world-class museum that has over 50,000 visitors each year, the Soulsville Foundation consists of the Stax Music Academy, a hugely successful, intensive after-school and summer music program whose students perform nationally and internationally and whose graduates have gone onto secondary music educations at renown programs, including the Berklee College of Music in Boston and its graduate school in Valencia, Spain. In 2005 the Soulsville Charter School was founded. Since 2012, when it held its first graduation, all of its seniors have been accepted to colleges and universities across the country with some form of scholarship or grant.

Surely the success of Stax and other arts organizations that preserve and progress Memphis' rich authentic cultural history and heritage throughout the city are worth celebrating. FunkyLux brought together Memphis' chefs, musicians, civic leaders and friends in celebration of the city's unique past and in support of its promising possibilities for the future. And while Stax is sending young musicians around the globe to hone their trade and share their talents, they will always have the soul of the Memphis Sound embedded in their spirits.

> "Soul food, soul music. The Bo-Keys are the best soul music band in the world. I love Memphis music and soul music. I gave them a call and sold them on the idea."
> –Brown Burch

With the Memphis Slim House as a backdrop, the chefs alley kitchen was soul in motion.

Chefs Ben Smith, Brown Burch

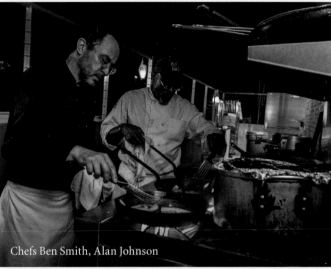

Chefs Ben Smith, Alan Johnson

Ellie Mascioli, Erin Sayle, and husband Henry Sayle, David Richardson

"I still think it's hilarious that we had an alcoholic amuse-bouche. We thought 'this is a party, we're going to party', we started out with a shooter."
–Jennifer Dickerson

The Bo-Keys and food for the soul.
L to r: Kirk Smothers, Marc Franklin, Howard Grimes, Archie Turner

DJ Witnesse

Ben Smith's fried oyster dish with rémoulade and fish eggs.

Chef Ben Smith's Pompano with sauce and hash.

Chef Brown Burch's "Memphis Soul Stew"

Stylist, Augusta Campbell

L to r: Anna Wunderlich, Ed Flemmons, Terri Flemmons, Cliff Hunt

Brave Design vintage inspired necklaces, blouses from Flashback Vintage. L to r: Maggie Swett, Augusta Campbell

A wall of hits: Server, Scott Miles. One of the many volunteer staff who worked from 5:00 pm to midnight to support the arts.

Express yourself in the photo booth. Ben Wunderlich and wife Anna, JJ Keras.

Bri Rogers, Leila Marten

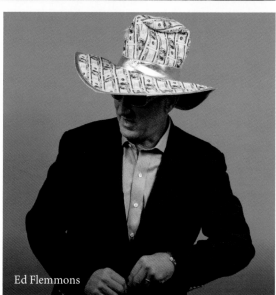

Ed Flemmons

The ultimate and infamous soul men, The Bo-Keys. L to r: Art Edmaiston, Marc Franklin, Scott Bomar, Percy Wiggins, Archie Turner

Just Chillin'. L to r: Ben Smith and Alan Johnson, chef by day and bass player for soul band, The Plantation Allstars, by night.

Listen to The Bo-Keys and work that skirt.
L to r: Lucia Heros, Anna Wunderlich, JJ Keras

Greg Baudoin, Lucia Heros

WASABI DEVILED EGGS

BEN SMITH

- 2 TABLESPOONS WASABI POWDER
- 2 TABLESPOONS WATER
- 12 EGGS
- 1½ TEASPOONS MUSHROOM SOY
- 1 CUP MAYONNAISE

In a bowl; mix wasabi powder and water to make a smooth paste. Cover and set aside for later.

Place whole eggs in an even layer in a saucepan. Add enough cold water to cover.

Bring to a boil on high heat. Cover the pan, remove from the heat and allow eggs to sit in the hot water for 15 minutes. Drain and cool eggs. When cool, peel and cut in half lengthwise.

Grate yolks on the small holes of a box grater or push them through a fine sieve.

In a bowl; mix together wasabi paste, mushroom soy and mayonnaise.

Place in a piping bag or a zip lock bag with the corner cut out and portion equally into all of the egg halves.

PORK AND LEMON GRASS MEATBALLS

BEN SMITH

- 1 POUND GROUND PORK
- 2 SHALLOTS, MINCED
- 3 CLOVES GARLIC, MINCED
- 2 TABLESPOONS CHOPPED LEMON GRASS
- ¼ CUP CHOPPED CILANTRO
- 1 EGG, LIGHTLY BEATEN
- ½ CUP PANKO BREAD CRUMBS
- 1 JALAPEÑO PEPPER, CHOPPED
- 1 TEASPOON FISH SAUCE
- 1 TEASPOON SALT

In a bowl; mix all ingredients together until blended well. Portion using a small ice cream scoop.

Roll into balls and place in a baking pan. Refrigerate for at least 1 hour before cooking.

Dredge in seasoned flour with plenty of fresh ground black pepper and sauté in batches until well browned on all sides. Place in baking pan and bake in a 350 degree oven until cooked through.

CHILLED AVOCADO SOUP

BEN SMITH

- 5 RIPE AVOCADOS
- JUICE OF 1 LEMON
- JUICE OF 1 LIME
- 10 OUNCES PLAIN, NON-FAT YOGURT
- 1¼ CUPS HALF-AND-HALF
- 1¼ CUPS VEGETABLE OR CHICKEN STOCK
- ½ TEASPOON TOASTED, GROUND CUMIN SEEDS
- 1 SMALL RED ONION, PEELED AND DICED FINE
- SALT, TO TASTE

Peel and pit avocados and toss them together in a large bowl with lemon juice, lime juice and yogurt. Purée the mixture in a blender or food processor until smooth.

Add remaining ingredients, season to taste, and chill well before serving.

SWEET POTATO-LEMON GRASS SOUP

BEN SMITH

- 2 OUNCES UNSALTED BUTTER
- 1 SMALL YELLOW ONION, PEELED AND DICED
- 1 OUNCE CHOPPED LEMON GRASS
- 1 TABLESPOON CHOPPED GINGER
- 1 JALAPEÑO PEPPER, STEMMED AND CHOPPED
- 1 (14 OUNCE) CAN COCONUT MILK
- 2½ POUNDS SWEET POTATOES, PEELED AND CUT INTO LARGE CHUNKS
- 4 QUARTS WATER
- SALT, TO TASTE

Melt butter in heavy stockpot. Add onions, lemon grass, ginger, and jalapeños.

Cook, stirring, until onions begin to soften. Add coconut milk and stir well.

Add sweet potatoes and water. Bring to a boil, reduce to a simmer and cook until potatoes are soft. Purée in blender, season to taste with salt.

AHI POKE

BEN SMITH

- 1 POUND SUSHI GRADE YELLOWFIN TUNA
- 1 CUP PEELED, SEEDED AND DICED CUCUMBER
- ½ CUP CHOPPED RED OR GREEN ONION
- 3 TABLESPOONS SOY SAUCE
- 1 TEASPOON SESAME OIL
- 1¼ CUPS VEGETABLE OR CHICKEN STOCK
- ½ TEASPOON CRUSHED RED PEPPER
- JUICE OF 1 LEMON

Cut tuna into small dices and place in a container with a tight-fitting lid or zip lock bag. Add remaining ingredients and mix well.

Store in refrigerator for at least 2 hours or until well chilled.

FUNKY STAX DIRTY RICE ARANCINI

BROWN BURCH

- FLOUR FOR DREDGING, SEASONED TO TASTE
- 3 EGGS, BEATEN
- GROUND PANKO BREAD CRUMBS
- 10 TABLESPOONS BUTTER, CUBED, DIVIDED
- 3 CLOVES OF GARLIC, SMASHED
- 1 TABLESPOON FRESH THYME, LEAVES PICKED
- 3 POUNDS CHICKEN LIVERS, ORGANIC – (CLEANED – BY TRIMMING THE VEIN)
- SALT AND PEPPER
- 1 CUP FINELY DICED YELLOW ONION
- 3 TABLESPOONS OLIVE OIL
- 1 (16 OUNCE) BAG ARBORIO RICE
- 4 CUPS WHITE WINE
- 3 QUARTS HOT CHICKEN STOCK
- ½ CUP GRATED PARMESAN REGGIANO

NOTES:
I wanted to take dirty rice and make it something more. I love serving salty, fried bites to start a big, luxurious meal. Turning the classic southern soul dish of dirty rice into the classic Italian antipasti arancini seemed like a great idea.

FOR FUN PRESENTATION:
Serve dirty rice balls on a bed of grated Parmesan or raw Arborio rice.

Place seasoned flour, beaten eggs and ground panko bread crumbs in separate bowls. Set aside.

In a large sauté pan, heat 2 tablespoons of the butter until it begins to brown. Add smashed garlic cloves and thyme leaves for 30 seconds. Then add cleaned chicken livers. Season with salt and pepper. Cook until livers are brown on all sides and cooked through. Set aside to cool.

Purée liver mixture in a food processor until it is creamy and smooth. Set aside.

In a large bottom pot or "rondeau", sweat onion in olive oil until translucent 8-10 minutes over medium heat.

Add rice and stir with wooden spoon; cook for 2-3 minutes. Add white wine; cook and stir until wine is evaporated. Ladle 2 cups of hot chicken stock at a time and stir until liquid is absorbed. Then repeat process until rice is al dente and creamy.

Take off heat and stir in chicken liver purée, remaining 8 tablespoons cubed butter, and grated Parmesan Reggiano. Stir like crazy until everything is incorporated. Season risotto with salt and black pepper. Spread out on sheet tray and cool.

Once cooled, roll into small bite-size balls. Dip into seasoned flour then egg wash and then ground panko bread crumbs. Re-roll ball so it is a nice round uniform shape. Fry at 350 degrees in oil until golden brown.

FUNKY LUX APPLE MOONSHINE COCKTAIL

BROWN BURCH

NOTES:
Very simple, delicious drinkable cocktail (this flavored "moonshine" is only 40 proof). I paired this with the frog course because I thought the sweet apple flavor would pair great with the strong pungent mustard, caper, and herb flavors in the dish.

*If you have on hand, add a shot of the real deal white lightning moonshine to this drink to take it to the next level.

- 2 OUNCES APPLE PIE MOONSHINE COCKTAIL "OLE SMOKEY TENNESSEE MOONSHINE"
- 2 OUNCES MARTINELLI'S APPLE JUICE
- 1 OUNCE CRANBERRY JUICE
- 3 CUPS CRUSHED ICE
- CHILLED HIGH BALL GLASS

Mix apple moonshine, apple juice, cranberry juice and 2 cups of ice in shaker. Shake it until its shook.

Strain over 1 cup crushed ice in chilled glass.

STAX FUNKY FROG LEG RAGOÛT

BROWN BURCH

FROG LEG CONFIT:

- 5 POUNDS FROG LEGS – BIG ARKANSAS FROGS PREFERABLY
- ½ CUP THINLY SLICED GARLIC
- ½ CUP THINLY SLICED SHALLOT
- ¼ CUP SALT
- ¼ CUP SLIGHTLY CRUSHED BLACK PEPPERCORNS
- ¼ CUP FRESH THYME, PICKED
- 10 BAY LEAVES, CRUSHED
- 2 QUARTS DUCK FAT OR CANOLA OIL

Coat frog legs evenly with rest of the ingredients except duck fat or canola oil. Let marinate or cure for 12 hours.

After 12 hours gently rinse frog legs under cold running water to remove herbs and spices; pat dry.

Submerge frog legs in duck fat or canola oil and bake at 250 degrees for 2 hours or until meat easily comes away from the bone.

Let frog legs come to room temperature in the fat and then shred meat being sure to remove all bones, sinew, cartilage, and veins. Set aside meat and reserve bones.

FROG JUS:

- FROG BONES FROM CONFIT (RECIPE ABOVE)
- 1 SMALL ONION, QUARTERED
- 2 CARROTS, PEELED AND CUT INTO 1 INCH PIECES
- 2 CELERY STALKS, CUT INTO 1 INCH PIECES
- 5 CLOVES GARLIC
- 2 BAY LEAVES
- 10 SPRIGS OF THYME
- 2 QUARTS CHICKEN STOCK

Roast bones in a 350 degree oven until browned, approximately 45 minutes to 1 hour.

Roast vegetables, herbs, and spices until slightly browned and caramelized.

Put roasted frog bones and vegetables in a pot; cover with chicken stock. Bring to a boil, turn down to a simmer and slowly reduce liquid by half.

Strain through fine mesh sieve (chinois) and reserve.

FROG RAGOÛT:

- 1 CUP MINCED SHALLOT
- 1 CUP MINCED LEEK
- ½ CUP MINCED CELERY
- 3 TABLESPOONS CANOLA OIL
- ¼ CUP MINCED GARLIC
- 2 CUPS WHITE WINE
- 1 QUART FROG JUS
- 1 CUP HEAVY WHIPPING CREAM
- 1 CUP CRÈME FRAÎCHE
- ½ CUP DIJON MUSTARD
- ½ CUP MINCED CORNICHONS
- ½ CUP MINCED CAPERS
- SALT AND WHITE PEPPER, TO TASTE
- 2 CUPS CONFIT FROG MEAT (RECIPE ABOVE)
- 2 TABLESPOONS CHIFFONADE PARSLEY
- 2 TABLESPOONS MINCED CHIVES
- 3 TABLESPOONS MINCED TARRAGON
- 1 TABLESPOON APPLE CIDER VINEGAR

- CREAMY, STONE GROUND GRITS, FOR SERVING

Sauté shallot, leek, and celery in canola oil over medium heat for 5 minutes. Add garlic and cook another 3 to 5 minutes. Deglaze with white wine and reduce until wine is 90% reduced.

Add frog jus, whipping cream, crème fraîche, Dijon mustard, cornichons, and capers. Bring to a boil and simmer 20 minutes until sauce is thickened. Season with salt and white pepper to taste. Add frog meat and heat through.

Right before serving add parsley, chives, and tarragon. Finish ragoût with a splash of apple cider vinegar.

Serve over a bed of creamy stone ground grits. (For Stax dinner we added spiced roasted tomato purée to our grits to make a delicious late summer take on the ordinary butter and cream laced grits. It also added a good contrast in color with the red grits underneath the yellowish-white frog ragoût with green specks of herbs.)

Serve with Funky Lux Apple Moonshine Cocktail.

Makes 8 appetizers or 4 main course portions.

NOTE:
I wanted to do a very fancy French version on the classic soul dish stewed frog legs.

VANILLA-LOBSTER POT PIES WITH FENNEL

JENNIFER DICKERSON

BLACK PEPPER PIE DOUGH:

- 1¼ CUPS ALL-PURPOSE FLOUR
- 1 TEASPOON SALT
- ½ TEASPOON FRESHLY GROUND BLACK PEPPER
- 8 TABLESPOONS UNSALTED BUTTER (COLD, CUT INTO PIECES)
- 4 TABLESPOONS ICE WATER

FILLING:

- FINELY SLICED FENNEL, ONION, MUSHROOM, LEEK, TO MAKE 1 CUP
- 5 TEASPOONS MINCED GARLIC
- 2 TABLESPOONS BUTTER
- 2 TABLESPOONS FLOUR
- 1 CUP CREAM
- 2 TABLESPOONS SHERRY
- 1 VANILLA BEAN, SCRAPPED
- 5 CUPS LOBSTER STOCK
- SALT AND PEPPER, TO TASTE
- 1 CUP COOKED AND CHOPPED LOBSTER MEAT

Place flour, salt, and pepper in the bowl of a food processor, and pulse to combine. Add butter and process until the mixture resembles coarse crumbs. While the machine is running, gradually drizzle in water, processing until the dough comes together to form a ball.

Transfer the dough to a lightly floured surface and shape it into a flat disk. Wrap it in plastic wrap and refrigerate it for at least 1 hour or up to overnight.

Sauté vegetables and garlic in hot pan, lightly oiled, until mixture begins to wilt.

Add butter and once melted, add flour; stir well. Add cream, sherry, vanilla bean, and stock; stir well to incorporate. Season with salt and pepper, and cook until thick. Add cooked lobster meat.

Blind bake pie crust in mini tartlet shells for 8 minutes, add filling and cook for an additional 8 minutes. Serve warm.

SUMMER SALAD PANACHÉ

JENNIFER DICKERSON

CUCUMBER-TOMATO SALAD:

- 1 KIRBY CUCUMBER, HALVED LENGTHWISE AND THINLY SLICED
- 5 MEDIUM PLUM TOMATOES, HALVED LENGTHWISE, SEEDED, AND THINLY SLICED
- ¼ RED ONION, PEELED, HALVED LENGTHWISE, AND THINLY SLICED
- DRIZZLE OF SESAME OIL, ABOUT 1 TABLESPOON
- 2 SPLASHES RED WINE VINEGAR
- COARSE SALT AND BLACK PEPPER
- BLACK SESAME SEED

In a large salad bowl combine cucumbers, tomatoes and onion.

Whisk together the remaining ingredients and pour over cucumber mix, toss to coat. Serve immediately.

EDAMAME SUCCOTASH:

- 1½ CUPS FROZEN OR FRESH SHELLED EDAMAME (SEE INGREDIENT NOTE)
- 1 TABLESPOON CANOLA OIL
- ¼ CUP CHOPPED ONION
- ¼ CUP CHOPPED LEEK
- 2 CLOVES GARLIC, MINCED
- 2 CUPS CORN KERNELS
- 3 TABLESPOONS DRY WHITE WINE OR WATER
- 2 TABLESPOONS RICE VINEGAR
- 2 TABLESPOONS CHOPPED FRESH PARSLEY
- 2 TABLESPOONS CHOPPED FRESH TARRAGON
- ½ TEASPOON SALT
- FRESHLY GROUND PEPPER, TO TASTE

Cook edamame in a large saucepan of lightly salted water until tender, about 4 minutes or according to package directions. Drain well.

Heat oil in a large nonstick skillet over medium heat. Add onion, leeks and garlic; cook, stirring frequently, until vegetables start to soften, about 2 minutes.

Stir in corn, wine (or water) and edamame; cook, stirring frequently, for 4 minutes. Remove from the heat.

Stir in vinegar, parsley, tarragon, salt and pepper. Serve immediately.

INSIDE OUT TRUFFLED DEVIL EGGS:

- 8 HARD-BOILED EGGS
- ½ CUP MAYONNAISE
- 1 LARGE CLOVE GARLIC, GRATED
- ZEST OF 1 LEMON
- ½ CUP CRÈME FRAÎCHE OR SOUR CREAM
- 1 TABLESPOON WHITE TRUFFLE OIL
- KOSHER SALT AND FRESHLY GROUND PEPPER
- ½ CUP CHOPPED FRESH PARSLEY
- ¼ CUP FINELY CHOPPED FRESH ROSEMARY
- 1 TABLESPOON WHITE TRUFFLE OIL, FOR DRIZZLING

Prepare hard-boiled eggs.

Halve eggs lengthwise and transfer yolks to a mixing bowl. Set egg white halves on a platter, cover, and refrigerate.

With a fork, mash yolks to a smooth consistency. Add mayonnaise, grated garlic, lemon zest, crème fraîche or sour cream, truffle oil, salt, and pepper; mix until smooth. (You can also do this using an electric mixer with a whip attachment.) Taste and season accordingly.

Spoon the mixture into a pastry bag fitted with a plain or large star tip, then pipe the mixture evenly into the egg white halves. Or fill the eggs with a spoon, dividing the filling evenly.

Top each egg half with parsley and rosemary; drizzle with truffle oil.

BANANA-CHARDONNAY PUDDING

JENNIFER DICKERSON

- ½ CUP SUGAR
- 1 TABLESPOON CORNSTARCH
- ⅛ TEASPOON SALT
- 1½ CUPS MILK
- ½ CUP CHARDONNAY
- 3 EGG YOLKS, BEATEN
- 1 TEASPOON VANILLA
- 1 BANANA, SLICED
- FRESH MINT, OPTIONAL

Combine sugar, cornstarch, and salt in a saucepan.

Over medium heat, slowly add milk and chardonnay; stir until mixture comes to a boil. Cook for 2 minutes.

Temper egg yolks by adding a small amount of hot liquid, then return all to the saucepan. Cook until thickened, then remove from heat. Stir in vanilla and chill custard for 1 hour.

Just before serving, fold in banana slices. Garnish with mint if desired and Honeysuckle Whipped Cream.

HONEYSUCKLE WHIPPED CREAM:

- ½ QUART WHIPPING CREAM
- ½ CUP LAVENDER INFUSED POWDERED SUGAR
- ZEST OF 1 ORANGE
- VANILLA WAFERS

Whip cream with sugar and orange zest.

Top banana pudding with whipped cream and vanilla wafers.

HEMINGWAY'S TABLE

THE CONNECTION BETWEEN THE CULINARY AND LITERARY ARTS RUNS DEEP. Mastery of technique and style along with a deliberate choice of ingredients make for both literary classics and memorable meals. No author is more associated with the *bon vivant* lifestyle than Ernest Hemingway. From the bistros of Paris to the plains of Africa, the landscapes of his life inspired the stories in his work. Hemingway's Table was inspired by the author's time in Key West, transporting guests to a tropical escape complete with a seafood feast and a very cool "Pop"....even in the dead of winter.

Chefs Ryan Trimm of Sweet Grass and Southward Fare & Libations, Jonathan Magallanes of Las Tortugas Deli Mexicana and Keith Bambrick of McEwen's Memphis envisioned an event in July where they would serve fresh, chilled seafood, popsicles and a host of other dishes to refresh guests during the sweltering Memphis summer. The party was rescheduled for October and finally for frigid February. As Keith recounts, "The party was initially scheduled in the summertime, but we kept the concept even though it got rescheduled." Though February may seem a strange month to have a Key West-themed party, it was ultimately a boon for the event, transforming Southward Fare & Libations into a sold-out tropical oasis in the middle of a cold, dreary winter.

Guests took the cold weather in stride sporting the requisite attire: winter whites, seersucker and linen. Inspired by other times in Hemingway's life and his exotic African Savannah travels, some wore their safari best. As guests arrived, they were greeted by Southward's warming atmosphere and welcoming bar staff serving up a host of delicious drinks in the polished wood bar, the architectural antithesis of Hemingway's Key West haunt, Sloppy Joe's. If beer was the preferred drink for the hot and sultry summer setting, as it was for Hemingway on many a night in his favorite beer hall in Madrid, a cold one could be fished out of the pirogue beer boat.

"As I ate the oysters with their strong taste of the sea and their faint metallic taste that the cold white wine washed away, leaving only the sea taste and the succulent texture, and as I drank their cold liquid from each shell and washed it down with the crisp taste of the wine, I lost the empty feeling and began to be happy and to make plans."–Ernest Hemingway, *A Moveable Feast*

The elegant restaurant was transformed into an authentic tropical oasis, thanks to the design prowess of party stylist and owner of Spruce Shop, Selena McAdams. Her smart,

KEITH BAMBRICK

KEITH BAMBRICK is the Executive Chef at McEwen's Memphis. A self-trained chef, Keith began in the restaurant industry at Memphis restaurant Swig under the management of Patrick Reilly. He was Sous Chef of McEwen's before becoming the Executive Chef. He has been featured in the *Commercial Appeal, Southern Living* and *Memphis Magazine*.

JONATHAN MAGALLANES

JONATHAN MAGALLANES is the owner, chef and manager of Las Tortugas Deli Mexicana. A Memphis native, Jonathan has been in the restaurant business from an early age. After living in Florida, Jonathan moved back to Memphis to assist his father, Jose "Pepe" Magallanes, who opened Las Tortugas in 2003. Acclaimed for its authentic Mexican cuisine and emphasis on local ingredients, Las Tortugas and the Magallanes have been featured in the *Commercial Appeal, The Memphis Flyer, Memphis Magazine* and other local and regional publications.

RYAN TRIMM

RYAN TRIMM is the Executive Chef and owner of Sweet Grass, Sweet Grass Next Door and Southward Fare & Libations in Memphis. Originally from Pittsburgh, Pennsylvania, Ryan grew up in Memphis before studying English and business at Ole Miss. After working at 208 South Lamar in Oxford, Ryan studied at Johnson and Wales University in Charleston, South Carolina, and worked with Frank Lee at Slightly North of Broad. After working at the Grove Grill as the Chef de Cuisine from 2005 to 2010, he opened Sweet Grass, followed by Sweet Grass Next Door and eventually Southward Fare & Libations. Ryan was nominated for *Food and Wine's* Peoples' Best New Chef 2011.

"I'm a big believer in the arts. I think the arts educate people, give people a purpose and make a nicer environment to live in. When people enjoy what they do, it's good for the city." –Ryan Trimm

Ryan Trimm and the succulent oysters.

Banana leaf, with wahoo steamed to perfection.

Jonathan Magallanes

Keith Bambrick's contagious enthusiasm.
L to r: Ryan Trimm, Keith Bambrick

Banana leaf collaboration wrapped up.
L to r: Ryan Trimm, Keith Bambrick

"The décor, the music, the ambiance—Selena made it all work with the food to take people away to an island." –Jonathan Magallanes

simplistic aesthetic was literally apparent with her menu design, a sepia toned, typewritten library catalogue card customized for each guest.

Propcellar, a vintage rental company founded and owned by Memphian Karlee Hickman, who has a background in interior design and merchandising, provided an imaginative inventory of vintage furniture and a natural flair for the unexpected.

As Ryan recounts, "We wanted to tie the party in with the arts. I was a literature major, and I'm a big fan of Mr. Hemingway, so that was something I really tuned into. Once Selena and I started talking about it, we got really into it."

The chefs gave their time generously and passionately to the dinner. Ryan and Keith were Culinary Series alumni, each participating in the 2012 dinner parties held in private homes. They both agreed to do it again, and Jonathan, new to the dinner series, came on board without hesitation. As Ryan explains, "I'm a big believer in the arts. Some people overlook culture and the arts, not only in educational systems, but also in communities themselves. I think they educate people, give people a purpose and make a nicer environment to live in. When people enjoy what they do and where they live, it's good for the city."

The dinner was highly collaborative, and the chefs all agreed that they enjoyed working as a team. Jonathan describes the collaborative nature of the dinner and the Culinary Series enthusiastically, "This model offered something new and different, and at the same time, it strengthened the chef community. Chefs are a subset of the artistic community in Memphis. We always want to put our best foot forward.

I was really humbled to be asked to participate with two amazingly talented chefs. Keith has such a meticulous approach, and Ryan comes with such big ideas and concepts. It's inspiring to see how they tackle things."

Keith also enjoyed the sense of camaraderie in the planning and execution of the meal. "We met three times beforehand to plan the meal. I thought the dinner turned out really well. The vibe was cool and everyone had a great time. It was all very stress-free." This laidback, stress-free vibe in the kitchen carried over throughout the evening and made for a festive, free-spirited event full of good conversation and hearty laughter.

The meal began with passed appetizers that included shrimp cocktail, calamari and of course, oysters: fried in cornmeal and Blue Point on the half shell. After pre-dinner libations and bites, guests sat down at long, gracious tables adorned with oversized palm fronds and orchids. For the main event, the chefs served a trio of ceviche followed by steamed wahoo, artfully presented in a

banana leaf. For dessert, chefs presented adult popsicles, creating a buzz with the boozy, frozen confections.

As Jonathan describes the meal, "The whole concept was an escape. It was sort of using food as a way to transport you to a very specific time and a place. With the concept of escape, we wanted to go as far away as possible in the dead of winter. We struck up on the idea of something that had no meat and that was all fresh, exotic ingredients, fruits and vegetables. To me that felt decadent in the good way. When you think of Hemingway you think of someone who was decadent in the best way possible."

Hemingway was known to favor and frequent certain cities around the globe, most notably Paris, Havana, Key West and especially, Madrid. To honor this passion, the entertainment for the evening began with the strings of Spanish guitarist Roy Brewer and ended with the final stomp of the New Ballet Ensemble & School's Noelia Garcia Carmona's traditional flamenco dance. The beautiful, contagious high-energy performance and the challenging, complex rhythms kept the crowd excited late into the meal.

The evening did have to come to end eventually, but not before the chefs left the kitchen to take questions from guests. All of the chefs spoke of exciting developments in the Memphis culinary scene and the sense of support they feel. As Jonathan remembers, "Memphis is awesome. I think many chefs in this city embrace our underdog role. It's great to have an underground culinary scene. Part of what's so exciting about the culinary scene in Memphis is that it's emerging."

Though they had to leave the warmth of Southward and the oasis that was Hemingway's Table, guests left with fond memories and in high spirits. To quote Hemingway himself from *A Movable Feast*, "We ate well and cheaply and drank well and cheaply and slept well and warm together and loved each other." By the end of the night, all were in agreement with that sentiment.

Selena's literal menu design, a typewritten author's catalogue card.

AUTHOR
Kathy Fish

TITLE
Hemingway's Table

DUE DATE
Feb. 9

MENU

APPETIZERS
SHRIMP COCKTAIL
CORNMEAL FRIED GULF OYSTERS,
caviar dressing
CALAMARI
BLUE POINT OYSTERS ON THE 1/2 SHELL

FIRST COURSE
TRIO OF CEVICHE:
Halibut, green chili, grapefruit
Sea Scallops, key lime, avocado
Crab, chayote, cilantro

ENTRÉE
WAHOO wrapped in a
banana leaf, chilled quinoa, lime

DESSERT
POPCICLES

Refreshing fare transports guests to an exotic place.

L to r: Chefs Keith Bambrick and Jonathan Magallances

Quinoa and steamed wahoo in banana leaf.

Ceviche in a frozen coconut with toasted cashews and green chile.

Transporting teetering coconut bowls.

The popular pirogue oyster and beer boat.

Specialty summer breeze cocktails.

David House, Emily House

L to r: Bob Craddock, Diane Mall

Sam Buckmaster, Joanna Foster, Bob McEwen

L to r: Justin Fox Burks and wife, Amy Lawrence

Paula Naidu

Selena McAdams, David McAdams

Paula Naidu, Sri Naidu

Margot McNeely and husband Gary Backaus

Lucy Lee

L to r: Jimmy Gould, Katie Smythe, Barry Lichterman, Carrie Pohlman Vaughan

Ham Smythe

Deborah Craddock and her husband Bob, Kathy Fish

Tricia and husband John Pontius, Sally Thomason

Kelly Fish and the "pops" of frozen color.

Jimmy Gould, Tom Lee, Ham Smythe, Julia Smythe

Seated, left to right: Sri Naidu, Paula Naidu, Andrew Ruhland, Carrie Ruhland, Megan Kerr, Emily House, David House, Maryl Smith, Joel Smith
Standing: David McAdams, Selena McAdams

Ryan Trimm

Q & A with the chefs: Chip Maley, Jonathan Magallanes, Keith Bambrick

L to r: Noella Garcia Carmona, guitarist, Roy Brewer

CONCH FRITTERS WITH PICKLED TARTAR SAUCE

KEITH BAMBRICK

- 1 CUP ALL-PURPOSE FLOUR
- 2 CUPS MASA
- 4 TEASPOONS BAKING POWDER
- 4 CUPS BUTTERMILK
- 4 LARGE EGGS
- HOT SAUCE OR SRIRACHA, TO TASTE
- 2 POUNDS CLEANED CONCH MEAT
- ½ EACH RED, YELLOW, AND POBLANO PEPPERS AND ½ RED ONION, ALL FINELY DICED
- ½ CUP SLICED SCALLIONS
- 2 TEASPOONS MINCED GARLIC
- SALT AND PEPPER, TO TASTE
- OIL FOR FRYING

In a large bowl, combine flour, masa, and baking powder. In a separate bowl, combine buttermilk, eggs, and hot sauce. Mix dry ingredients and buttermilk mixture together.

Fold in conch meat, vegetables, and salt and pepper; let rest for 30 minutes. (Mixture should be pretty thick but not doughy. Add buttermilk if too thick and flour if too thin.) Roll into 2-ounce balls.

In a skillet or fryer, heat oil. Oil should be about 2 to 3 inches deep. With a large spoon or handled scoop, drop fritters into oil. Cook until golden, turning once. Serve with Pickled Pepper Tartar Sauce.

PICKLED PEPPER TARTAR SAUCE:

- 1 CUP MAYONNAISE
- ¼ CUP PICKLE RELISH
- 3-4 PICKLED HOT PEPPERS, MINCED
- ½ TEASPOON MINCED GARLIC
- DASH OF HOT SAUCE
- SALT AND PEPPER, TO TASTE

Mix all ingredients together; add salt and pepper to taste.

SCALLOP CEVICHE WITH AVOCADO AND KEY LIME

KEITH BAMBRICK

- 2 POUNDS LARGE FRESH SEA SCALLOPS CLEANED OF ATTACHMENT
- JUICE OF 15 KEY LIMES OR MORE
- JUICE OF 6 LEMONS
- 2 TO 3 MEDIUM AVOCADOS, DICED
- 2 SHALLOTS, THINLY SLICED
- 4 RADISHES, THINLY SLICED
- 1 BUNCH CILANTRO, CHOPPED
- 1 FINGER FRESH GINGER, FINELY MINCED
- 1 TEASPOON FINELY MINCED GARLIC
- 2 TEASPOONS SRIRACHA
- 1 SEEDLESS CUCUMBER, FINELY DICED
- 2 TABLESPOONS EXTRA VIRGIN OLIVE OIL TO COAT
- SALT AND PEPPER, TO TASTE

Thinly slice scallops (3-4 slices per scallop) and marinate in juice. Make sure scallops are covered by the liquid. Cover and refrigerate.

After 1 hour, uncover and check scallops. They should have started to turn a little opaque. If not, marinate a little longer.

Add all of the other ingredients and toss. Season with salt and pepper to taste.

Serve the ceviche on fried wontons, on a salad, or just with a spoon.

FROZEN COCONUT CEVICHE

JONATHAN MAGALLANES

Serves 8

- 4 WHITE COCONUTS
- 1 CUP PINEAPPLE JUICE
- 32 OUNCES GULF SHRIMP
- 1 MEDIUM CUCUMBER, DISCARD SEEDS
- 1 SMALL RED ONION
- 1 JALAPEÑO PEPPER, DISCARD SEEDS
- 1 SMALL JICAMA
- 2 MANGOES
- JUICE OF 6 LIMES
- JUICE OF 3 ORANGES
- ½ TEASPOON KOSHER SALT
- ½ TABLESPOON DRIED OREGANO
- ½ CUP ROASTED CASHEWS
- ½ CUP MACADAMIA NUTS
- 1 BUNCH CILANTRO

Slice coconuts in half with a saw, reserve coconut juice.

Fill each coconut with ⅛ cup of pineapple juice and place in freezer.

Bring water to a boil in a large sauce pot. Stir in shrimp. Return to boil. Cover and cook 2 minutes or until shrimp turn pink. Remove from heat and let stand 2 minutes. Drain well.

Peel and devein shrimp. Butterfly and chop shrimp into ¼-inch pieces. Place chopped shrimp into a glass bowl.

Peel and chop cucumber, red onion, jalapeño pepper, jicama, and mango into ¼-inch pieces into a glass bowl.

Add lime juice and reserved coconut juice to the chopped shrimp. Stir. Chill.

Add orange juice to the chopped fruit vegetable mixture. Stir and chill. Let all ingredients chill overnight in the refrigerator.

Remove all refrigerated ingredients. Strain shrimp mixture and fruit vegetable mixture. Add shrimp to the fruit vegetable mixture and toss with salt and oregano. Let mixture chill for 1 hour.

Remove frozen coconuts from freezer and add desired quantity of ceviche inside the shell. Garnish with nuts and cilantro.

QUINOA SALAD

RYAN TRIMM

Yields 4 servings

- 2 TABLESPOONS OLIVE OIL
- 1 CUP QUINOA, RINSED IN A SIEVE AND DRAINED WELL
- 1 GARLIC CLOVE, MINCED
- 2 CUPS WATER
- PINCH OF SALT OR MORE
- 2 LIMES, ZEST AND JUICED
- ½ CUP SLICED SCALLION
- 2 TABLESPOONS CHIFFONADE BASIL
- 2 TABLESPOONS CHOPPED CILANTRO
- 1 TABLESPOON CHIFFONADE MINT
- SALT AND PEPPER, TO TASTE

Heat a large frying pan to medium-high heat, add olive oil and warm slightly. Add quinoa and cook until golden.

Add garlic and cook for 2 minutes.

Add water and a little more than a pinch of salt. Cook until water is absorbed.

Spread out on a baking sheet to cool.

Add cooled quinoa and next 5 ingredients to a mixing bowl and mix well. Add salt and pepper to taste.

PALETA DE HORCHATA

JONATHAN MAGALLANES

Makes 24 popsicles

- 11 cups water
- 2 cups uncooked long-grain white rice
- 1 small 4 inch portion Mexican cinnamon (can be found in latin markets)
- 1¼ cups 2% milk
- 1¼ cups granulated sugar
- 1 tablespoon vanilla extract

Combine water and rice in a Vitamix or similar blender. Blend for about 30 to 45 seconds or until rice begins to break up. Chill in the refrigerator overnight.

Strain rice water into a large jug or pitcher and discard rice.

Toast cinnamon in a dry skillet until well toasted and fragrant. (There may be a few charred or dark spots.)

Grind cinnamon in a mortar until it is like dust. Or place in a food processor and finely grind cinnamon into powder.

Add milk, sugar, vanilla and cinnamon into rice milk. Stir vigorously and chill.

Remove from refrigerator and stir again. Add to popsicle molds and freeze.

Note:
Mixture may settle as it freezes but will not affect the flavor.

COCONUT POPSICLES

RYAN TRIMM

POPSICLES:

- 28 ounces full fat coconut milk
- 4 tablespoons honey
- juice of 1 lime
- 2 ounces powdered gelatin

Heat coconut milk, honey, gelatin and lime juice until honey is dissolved. Allow to cool and pour into popsicle molds.

Cover and place in freezer.

Once cooled, make the chocolate ganache.

GANACHE:

- 8 ounces bittersweet chocolate
- ½ cup heavy cream

Place bittersweet chocolate and heavy cream in a double boiler and melt together.

Once combined, gently dip coconut popsicles in ganache and lay out on wax paper on a baking sheet; put back in the freezer (it helps to put the baking sheet in the freezer 20 minutes before serving).

Feel free to add chopped nuts or toasted coconut shavings to top of wet chocolate.

Cover and place in freezer.

HOMEGROWN
TREASURES

WHILE MEMPHIS LITERALLY SITS AT THE CONFLUENCE OF THE MISSISSIPPI AND WOLF RIVERS, its soul sits at the confluence of a rich artistic and cultural legacy. Memphis is a city like no other. Whether it's the fertile soil of the Mississippi Delta or Memphis' renowned aquifer, it seems that there is just something in the water that makes it a city overflowing with authenticity. Both the place and the arts are unique—Memphis throws its elbows when it dances fast, and it swings its hips when it dances slow. The city's past has bestowed its present with a bounty of Homegrown Treasures—the inspiration for this event.

From its inspiring spot on the bluffs of the Mississippi River, an artery of commerce and culture for centuries, the Hyde Family Foundations provided the perfect setting for the evening. While the Hyde family's legacy of philanthropy dates back to the early 20th century, the Foundation was founded by Joseph Reeves Hyde, Sr. in 1961 with the mission to build a better Memphis through family-driven philanthropy. Today Hyde's grandson, Pitt, and his wife Barbara, along with their family members, lead the Foundations and are committed to transforming Memphis into a model city of the 21st century. The Foundations have contributed to Memphis' downtown revitalization by providing an accessible and impressive venue for community-wide philanthropy.

While the Foundations are involved in a wide variety of initiatives, from education to community development to greening Memphis, Homegrown Treasures showcases the Foundations' support of Memphis' unforgettable and indispensable artistic and cultural assets. Pitt explains, "Our family, like many others, believes that arts institutions are an essential component of a vibrant city, and in Memphis a thriving arts community is the cornerstone of our city's cultural capital. The arts are also one of our city's biggest competitive advantages and they contribute immensely to Memphis' economic and social vitality."

Spicy, sweet and a little greasy was the order of the entertainment menu. Ballet Memphis dancers performed to a juicy, jump-to-your-feet, iconic Memphis Stax soul standard "Green Onions." The Hattiloo Theatre, the region's only black repertory theatre company, gave a big nod to our rock and roll heritage with excerpts from the magnetic musical, Grease. The performances represented the history of the Hydes' support for the arts in Memphis. Hyde Family Foundations Program Director, Gretchen McLennon explains, "The first arts organization the Hydes supported was Ballet Memphis under the leadership of Dorothy Gunther Pugh, and one of the newest groups is the Hattiloo Theatre under the leadership of Ekundayo Bandele. The performances show the breadth and scope of our portfolio and arts patronage, as well as the great things arts organizations are doing today."

Melodye Ruby, the Foundations Events Coordinator, explains, "Memphis is incredibly fortunate to have so many art mediums, from exquisite dining with locally sourced ingredients to the raw beat of the blues, from talented dance troupes to graffiti and old masters. And the magnificent sunsets over Ole Man River with the 'Big M' bridging east and west in the forefront, all of these assets are here for individuals to explore and enjoy. We wanted to showcase as many art forms as possible and have art 'pop-out' throughout the evening."

Erick New from Garden District expertly styled the setting for the evening. He explains his inspiration behind the refined,

ANDREW ADAMS

ANDREW ADAMS is the Executive Chef at ACRE Restaurant in Memphis, Tennessee. He began his career as an apprentice at KC's Restaurant in Cleveland, Mississippi, where he cooked with Chef Wally Joe for three years. After attending the Culinary Institute of America, he worked with Chef Jamie Shannon at Commander's Palace in New Orleans, and later with Chef Craig Shannon at the Ryland Inn in Whitehouse, New Jersey. In 2002 he returned to Memphis to help open Wally Joe Restaurant and later ACRE Restaurant.

JUSTIN FOX BURKS & AMY LAWRENCE

JUSTIN FOX BURKS and AMY LAWRENCE are the husband and wife team behind the much-loved blog, The Chubby Vegetarian, and the 2013 cookbook, *The Southern Vegetarian*. Justin is a photographer whose food photography has appeared in *Food & Wine, Garden & Gun, Mojo, Memphis Magazine* and the *London Independent*. He writes for *Edible Memphis* and the *Memphis Flyer*. Amy is a food writer whose work has appeared in *Memphis Magazine, Edible Memphis* and the *Memphis Flyer*.

"We were inspired by the Foundation's art collection. For the Carroll Cloar S'more, we saw the sunflower and were inspired to add sunflower seeds to the s'more crust, which is made from my wife's sugar cookie recipe. We also chose color and form from Nancy Cheairs' paintings, and created the 'Nancy Cheairs soda.' The shape of the people she drew reminded us of the shape of a soda bottle, and we used her forms and colors for the label."

—Justin Fox Burks

Pitt Hyde

All natural beauty.

Justin Fox Burks forages for the freshest.

Efficiency is the key.

Andrew Adams, headed for the river bluff.

elegant, yet simple, décor, "When Melodye called me about the party we decided to keep it simple since we were working with a wonderful view of the river. We incorporated lighting to wash the event in sunset colors and used natural fabrics on the tables in order not to compete with the amazing view from the bluff."

Pitt treated guests to a tour of his personally curated collection of contemporary art, a truly special and memorable experience. The collection shows Pitt's intention to showcase his beloved city through local art.

The Hydes' art collection spans their homes in Memphis, New York City and Aspen as well as the Pittco Offices in Memphis. Barbara remarks that Pitt's love of art has been a "nourishing and balancing force in his life," and that collecting art was their "first joint endeavor" that began at the start of their relationship over 20 years ago.

The other artists in culinary action for the party were chefs Amy Lawrence, Justin Fox Burks and Andrew Adams, who created an artistically inspired, flexitarian feast celebrating the Mid-South's bounty of homegrown treasures. Inspired by the Foundations' art collection, Justin describes the process behind their creations, "We did a tour and instantly connected with some of the paintings. We didn't necessarily take the piece of art and recreate it on the plate because that would have been too obvious. We decided to take an idea from the painting and went through a few iterations. We were able to make those connections between what we were doing and what we saw on the wall."

The region's literal homegrown treasures, the products of its rich Delta farmlands, also inspired the chefs. Andrew, chef of ACRE Restaurant in Memphis and Justin, half of the husband and wife duo behind The Chubby Vegetarian blog and cookbook *The Southern Vegetarian*, both grew up on farms in rural Mississippi and used the evening to highlight the importance of Memphis' agrarian heritage in its cuisine. They devised the concept of a flexitarian menu as a natural extension of their lifestyles and as a way to make all of the guests happy. As Andrew explains, "When I'm at home 99% of the time, I cook vegetarian or pescetarian. This is very much the way I eat. I'm a flexitarian. This is right up my alley, and these are the

flavors I like." Amy remarks that, "Making vegetarian versions of the dishes and how they would echo their counterparts was exciting. We eat so much great, healthy food at home, and I want to share that way of enjoying food with others." And guests certainly flexed their culinary muscles as they reached for the wide variety of dishes that they experienced-from kombu- cured watermelon crudo to yakatori.

These creations were greatly appreciated by the guests, and Amy remembers the gracious feel of the evening, "That night, we met dedicated culinary students and their encouraging instructors who made this dinner happen for us; the happy guests who loved our food; and all the people from the Hyde Foundations and ArtsMemphis who helped our vision land on its feet at the event. Appreciation is so important. I felt that we were around people who loved our food and were excited by what we created for them. It made me realize that what we are trying to do in terms of food in Memphis is recognized and supported."

As Andrew explains, "The roots of the food — our homegrown treasures — are very much what we do. I grew up in a town of 10,000, and I worked on our farm. For me, homegrown treasures are what we experienced and what we ate."

Justin adds, "Amy and I are flexitarian, so this just made sense because it offers two ways to cook something to make everybody happy."

Andrew's co-chefs agree that Memphis' cuisine is authentic. Justin explains, "The focus does come from the ground up, from our mothers and grandmothers who taught us how to cook the family recipes and the things we eat at family gatherings. In Memphis the culinary tradition seeps up from our roots; it really does trickle up. In other cities it trickles down. And that's the difference between Memphis and every other city."

As for the future of the culinary arts in Memphis, Andrew predicts that big things are in store. "I have been here for eleven years," he says "and I have seen that you can really go around this city and eat some fantastic food—and not just the fine dining restaurants but everywhere. The home cooks here are really ahead of the curve." Justin adds, "What's so exciting about Memphis, including and beyond the culinary arts, is that it doesn't fit into a neat box."

The word that comes to mind when describing Memphis' culture, from its music to the culinary arts to the urban landscape, is authenticity. And thanks to a dedicated group of artists, philanthropists, civic leaders and everyday Memphians working hard to ensure that these assets are properly celebrated, supported and perpetuated, our city's cultural future looks very bright indeed.

Andrew Adams and Justin Fox Burks, culinary works of art.

Homegrown Treasures

BALLET MEMPHIS, HATTILOO THEATRE, MEMPHIS COLLEGE OF ART,
HYDE FAMILY FOUNDATIONS ART COLLECTION

BEAUTY

Jim Spake on Saxophone & Joe Restivo on Guitar

7:00 p.m.
Performance from *Grease* by Hattiloo Theatre

8:00 p.m.
Performance of *Running Ahead of Fate* by Ballet Memphis

Self-guided tours of the Hyde Family Foundations art
collections throughout the evening

7:30 p.m.
Guided art tour led by Pitt Hyde

8:15 p.m.
Guided art tour led by Billy Sights

Derrick Dent, Memphis College of Art instructor
capturing the evening on canvas

To learn more about the artists you're supporting this evening, please
visit **artsmemphis.org/homegrown** for stories from some of our city's
favorite arts groups.

"Making vegetarian versions of the dishes and how they echo their counterparts was exciting. We eat so much great healthy food at home and I want to share that way of enjoying food with others." –Amy Lawerence

An ode to the green movement.

"In Memphis a thriving arts community is the cornerstone of our city's cultural capitol. The arts are also one of our city's biggest competitive advantages and they contribute immensely to Memphis' economic and social vitality." –Pitt Hyde

Andrew Adams and Justin Fox Burks in the Hyde Family Foundations' kitchen.

Andrew Adams enlists the help of a Boys and Girls Club culinary student.

Berber spiced tomato nachos with fresh Farmer's cheese. Chips are made from injera, a fermented Ethiopian flatbread, that has been fried.

Signature soda.

L to r: Kathy Fish, Margot McNeely, Justin Fox Burks

L to r: Andrew Seamons, Carol Seamons, Pitt Hyde

Pravi Thakkar digging in.

Steve Lawrence samples the steamed buns.

Sea Island Pea Salad, Grilled Romaine Hearts, Cornbread, Shaved Parmesan.

Hattiloo Theatre performs *Grease*, backdrop: Mississippi River.

The Pink Ladies dance the night away.

L to r: Kate Thakkar, Pravi Thakkar, Blandy Lawrence

Our most authentic homegrown treasure: the Mississippi River at twilight.

Collecting art began as Pitt and Barbara's first joint endeavor over 20 years ago.

Pitt shares his vast knowledge and provenance of his art collection.

Chef Andrew Adams and Barbara Hyde.

Chef Andrew Adams

L to r: Amy Lawrence, Andrew Adams and Justin Fox Burks, also known as The Chubby Vegetarian serve up laughs.

Ballet Memphis dancers trade their slippers for sneakers. Dancers.
L to r: Crystal Brothers, Kendall Britt, Elizabeth Mensah, Stephanie Mei Hom and Brandon Ramey

Barbara Hyde working tirelessly to make a difference in Memphis.

L to r: Joe Restivo, Jim Spake

Barbara Mulligan and Chris Cooley

L to r: Justin Taylor, Steve Lawrence, Lauren Taylor, Alan Gates

Derrick Dent

Memphis College of Art alum and professor Derrick Dent contributed to the entertainment by capturing the evening with a series of free hand drawings of guests.

Gretchen McLennon, Hyde Family Foundations Program Director, a perfect subject for Derrick's artistry.

SMOKED EGGPLANT & DATE YAKITORI

JUSTIN FOX BURKS, AMY LAWRENCE AND ANDREW ADAMS

SPECIAL EQUIPMENT: ELECTRIC SMOKER, OUTDOOR GRILL, BAMBOO SKEWERS

- 1 LARGE ITALIAN EGGPLANT
- 1 TEASPOON KOSHER SALT
- 1 TABLESPOON SESAME OIL
- 1 TABLESPOON (UNSEASONED) RICE VINEGAR
- 20 PITTED DATES, APPROXIMATELY
- YAKITORI SAUCE (RECIPE FOLLOWS)
- TOGARASHI, TO GARNISH

Peel eggplant and cut in half. Slice each half into less than ¼ inch strips. Layer the strips of eggplant into a large glass bowl while salting each layer as you go. Allow eggplant to rest for at least 15 minutes. This will soften the eggplant and leach out any bitterness. Rinse eggplant under cold water and then gently squeeze out any moisture — just like squeezing the water from a washcloth.

Fire up the smoker to 175 degrees using hickory chunks for flavor.

Return eggplant strips to the bowl and add sesame oil and rice vinegar. Toss to coat. Lay strips out onto the trays and place into the preheated smoker for 6 minutes. Remove from smoker and set aside. (*If you do not have access to a smoker, simply add Liquid Smoke to your Yakitori Sauce.)

Fire up the outdoor grill to high. A charcoal grill is best here, but gas is fine. Thread eggplant strips and whole, pitted dates onto the skewers (see photos). You should get about 9 double skewers or 18 smaller, single skewers. Grill for about 5 minutes per side or until well-marked by the grill grates. Make sure to hang the sticks off of the hot part of the grill or protect them with a strip of foil so they don't burn up.

Dip in or brush on the yakitori sauce. Garnish with togarashi. Serve immediately. Serves 6 as an appetizer or 2 as a meal with some rice.

YAKITORI SAUCE

- ½ CUP SOY SAUCE
- ½ CUP MIRIN (SWEET JAPANESE COOKING WINE)
- ½ CUP VEGETABLE STOCK
- 2 CLOVES GARLIC, SMASHED
- 1 TEASPOON LIQUID SMOKE (IF YOU DO NOT HAVE ACCESS TO A SMOKER)

Into a medium saucepan, place soy sauce, mirin, stock, and garlic (and optional Liquid Smoke) over medium-low heat until reduced by a third.

Set aside until ready to use.

KOMBU-CURED WATERMELON CRUDO + HOT PEPPERS & CHIVES

JUSTIN FOX BURKS, AMY LAWRENCE AND ANDREW ADAMS

Special equipment: food dehydrator and vacuum sealer (optional)

- 1 PERSONAL-SIZED SEEDLESS WATERMELON
- 4 PIECES KOMBU (DRIED SEAWEED, AVAILABLE AT WHOLE FOODS)
- JUICE FROM 2 LIMES
- 2 JALAPEÑO OR SERRANO PEPPERS, VERY THINLY SLICED
- GOOD-QUALITY OLIVE OIL, TO DRIZZLE OVER WATERMELON
- SNIPPED CHIVES, TO GARNISH
- SEA SALT FLAKES AND CRACKED BLACK PEPPER, TO TASTE

Cut watermelon into a large square by trimming off all of the sides to reveal the heart. Trim off any rind that remains. Cut into 2 x 2 x 4 inch blocks — you should get 4 from a small watermelon.

Place watermelon blocks into a 125-degree dehydrator for about 4 hours until the short side has reduced by roughly half; at this point, it should measure just over 1 inch. Briefly rinse kombu under cold water and place along the top and bottom of the dehydrated watermelon. Either vacuum seal or place into an airtight container in the refrigerate overnight.

Remove watermelon from container and discard kombu. Using a sharp knife, thinly slice each block of the watermelon and shingle onto a plate. Garnish each with ¼ of the lime juice, a few hot pepper slices, a drizzle of ¼ teaspoon of olive oil, a few chives, and salt and pepper. Serves 4 as a first course.

Three Graces
by Ted Faires

VEGETARIAN KOREAN BBQ MUSHROOM STEAMED BUNS

JUSTIN FOX BURKS, AMY LAWRENCE, AND ANDREW ADAMS

Do Ahead:
Make the Quick Asian Pickle and the Roasted Red Pepper Korean BBQ Sauce.

- 10 TO 12 FROZEN STEAMED BUNS (THE KIND THAT IS A FOLDED CIRCLE WITH A HINGE)
- 1 TEASPOON TOASTED SESAME OIL
- 2 TEASPOONS CANOLA OIL (LIKE WHOLE FOODS 365 BRAND)
- 4 CUPS (ABOUT A POUND) SLICED MUSHROOMS (CRIMINI, SHIITAKE)
- ROASTED RED PEPPER KOREAN BBQ SAUCE (RECIPE FOLLOWS)
- QUICK ASIAN PICKLE (RECIPE FOLLOWS)
- CHOPPED ROASTED PEANUTS, CHOPPED GREEN ONION, AND CILANTRO, TO GARNISH

Steam frozen buns in a parchment-lined bamboo steamer (or another method you can dream up) for 10-15 minutes or until each bun is soft and pliable. Hold in the bamboo steamer until ready to serve.

In a large pan over high heat, heat sesame oil and canola until they start to smoke. Add mushrooms to the pan in a single layer. Allow them to cook undisturbed for 3 minutes or until nicely browned on one side. Toss them around in the pan and cook for another 1-2 minutes until mushrooms appear to be heated through. Add Roasted Red Pepper Korean BBQ Sauce to the pan and toss to coat. Remove from heat and cover to keep warm until ready to serve.

To assemble, stuff each bun with about ¼ cup of the mushroom mixture, a few slices of Quick Asian Pickle, a sprinkling of chopped roasted peanuts, a few sliced green onions, and some cilantro.

Makes about 12 steamed buns.

QUICK ASIAN PICKLE

JUSTIN FOX BURKS, AMY LAWRENCE, AND ANDREW ADAMS

- 1 CUCUMBER, THINLY SLICED
- ½ CUP RICE VINEGAR
- ½ CUP WATER
- 1 TEASPOON KOSHER SALT
- 1 TABLESPOON CANE SUGAR
  (LIKE WHOLE FOODS 365 BRAND)

Place cucumber slices into a pint jar.

In a medium mixing bowl, whisk together vinegar, water, salt, and sugar.

Pour pickling liquid over cucumbers, place a lid on the jar, and refrigerate for at least 1 hour and up to a week.

ROASTED RED PEPPER KOREAN BBQ SAUCE

JUSTIN FOX BURKS, AMY LAWRENCE, AND ANDREW ADAMS

- 2 MEDIUM ROASTED RED PEPPERS,
  STEMMED, SEEDED
- 1 TABLESPOON CANE SUGAR
  (LIKE WHOLE FOODS 365 BRAND)
- 2 TABLESPOONS SOY SAUCE
- 1 TABLESPOON SAMBAL
- 1 TABLESPOON RICE VINEGAR
- 1 TEASPOON SESAME OIL
- ¼ TEASPOON POWDERED GINGER
- ¼ TEASPOON GRANULATED GARLIC
- WHITE (OR BLACK) CRACKED PEPPER, TO TASTE

Place roasted red pepper, sugar, soy sauce, sambal, rice vinegar, sesame oil, ginger, garlic, and pepper in a food processor and blend until smooth.

Store in an airtight container in the refrigerator for up to a week.

Makes about 1 cup of sauce.

VEGGIE CHORIZO TORTELLINI IN A SWEET PEA AND GINGER BROTH WITH SPROUTED RYE

JUSTIN FOX BURKS, AMY LAWRENCE AND ANDREW ADAMS

SPROUTED RYE:

NOTE:
This is a 3-day preparation process.

Soak ¼ cup rye seeds for 8 hours. Drain and place into bowl by a window with soft light. The next day, rinse, drain, and set it back in the window until little tails start to form. Cover and refrigerate until ready to use.

SWEET PEA AND GINGER BROTH:

- 1 POUND ENGLISH PEAS (1 BAG FROZEN)
- 1 (4-INCH) PIECE GINGER
- 2 CUPS VEGETABLE BROTH
- ½ CUP HEAVY CREAM

In a blender, place peas, ginger, broth, and cream. Blend until smooth. Strain using a food mill. Set aside in the refrigerator until ready to use.

VEGETABLE-CHORIZO MIXTURE:

- 8 OUNCES CREMINI MUSHROOMS
- 1 LARGE RED BELL PEPPER
- 1 SMALL WHITE ONION
- 4 CLOVES GARLIC
- 1 TABLESPOON SMOKED PAPRIKA
- 1 TEASPOON CHILI FLAKES
- 1 TEASPOON CUMIN
- 1 TEASPOON CORIANDER
- ¼ TEASPOON OREGANO
- 2 TABLESPOONS SHERRY VINEGAR
- 2 TABLESPOONS OLIVE OIL,
  PLUS MORE FOR COOKING
- 1 TABLESPOON FERMENTED BLACK BEAN
  SAUCE
- ½ CUP BREAD CRUMBS
- 1 LARGE EGG, BEATEN
- 1 CUP GRATED SMOKED MOZZARELLA CHEESE
- KOSHER SALT AND CRACKED BLACK PEPPER,
  TO TASTE
- 2 BUNCHES BOK CHOY,
  CUT INTO BITE-SIZED PIECES
- MANCHEGO CHEESE, TO GARNISH

FRESH PASTA DOUGH:

- 1½ CUPS SEMOLINA FLOUR
- 2 LARGE EGGS
- 1 LARGE EGG YOLK
- PLUS 1 EGG, BEATEN, FOR BRUSHING
  PASTA SQUARES

Preheat the oven to 350 degrees. Using your food processor, pulse to finely chop the mushrooms, red pepper, onion, and garlic in batches; place them on a large parchment-lined, rimmed baking sheet. Add paprika, chili flakes, cumin, coriander, oregano, vinegar, olive oil, and fermented black bean paste. Using your hands, toss the ingredients to incorporate. Spread the mixture evenly on to the baking sheet and bake for 20 minutes. Allow the mixture to cool.

In a large mixing bowl, combine the spiced vegetable mixture with the bread crumbs, egg, and smoked mozzarella. Mix to incorporate. Add salt and pepper to taste. (It should be just slightly on the salty side since it'll be wrapped in pasta.) Set veggie chorizo mixture aside until you are ready to stuff the pasta.

In a large mixing bowl, add the flour and make a well in the center using your hands. Add eggs and yolk to the well; beat using a fork. Begin to incorporate flour by kneading the eggs into the flour. (All the flour will not be picked up by the eggs.) There will be some dry flour left in the bowl once the moisture from the eggs has picked up all it can. Knead dough until smooth, wrap in plastic, and set aside until ready to use.

On a well-floured countertop, using a pasta machine, roll out the pasta dough starting at a number one setting and working it down to a number five setting. Cut the strips in half lengthwise and then into squares using a pasta wheel; you should end up with roughly 40 squares. (See photos.)

Place about ¼ teaspoon of the veggie-chorizo mixture in the center of a square of pasta, pick it up, brush the edges with beaten egg, and fold it into a triangle. Then wrap two of the corners around your fingertip and pinch.

Finally, fold the unconnected corner up toward the filling to create a tortellini. Place on a well-floured baking sheet. Repeat process until all pasta is used up.

Bring a large pot of salted water to a boil and heat a large skillet to medium-high. Add a tablespoon of olive oil to the skillet and sauté the bok choy until tender. Cook pasta in the boiling water for 1 to 2 minutes or until it floats. Remove using a sieve and place directly into the pan with the bok choy. Add ½ cup of the sprouted rye. Toss to incorporate.

TO ASSEMBLE DISH:

Place 5-8 tortellini and some bok choy on each plate. Using an immersion blender, whir the Sweet Pea and Ginger Broth to foam it. Garnish with Sweet Pea and Ginger Broth and manchego cheese. Makes 5 to 8 servings.

NAPA CHIC

In the words of chef John Besh, "Eat Well. Do Good."
Napa Chic hosts Beni and Mike Dragutsky are old hats
at the school of entertaining with a purpose, connecting
a good cause around their celebratory common table.
They graciously opened their kitchen to chefs Jackson
Kramer and Nick Seabergh, their home to the Tennessee
Shakespeare Company and countless bottles of
memorable wine from their beloved Cornerstone Cellars
to create an evening that mirrored the winery's mantra,
Excellence Is Not Enough.

Beni and Mike are consummate hosts who connect their passions for philanthropy with their passions for wine, food, friends and general merriment. As owners of Cornerstone Cellars and Stepping Stone Cellars wineries in Napa Valley and Willamette Valley, Oregon, their healthy appetites for food and drink run deep. Having chaired the Memphis Brooks Museum of Art's Memphis Wine + Food Series, they recognize the relationship between more traditional types of art and emerging interests in the arts of food and wine. As Mike explains, "We got involved with supporting the arts through wine. There is a social and giving spirit with wine that crosses over to the arts and that is not often seen with other interests."

For party stylist Sheril Greenstein, a detail-oriented approach set the perfect atmosphere for the evening. Sheril has been an event planner for ten years as the owner of Shindigs by Sheril. As Sheril normally plans events for hundreds of people, a dinner party for twenty-four was a welcome occasion to focus on creating an intimate, personalized and magical evening. "I usually plan events for 300 people, so I was able to execute many more details with a smaller event," Sheril says. "We wanted guests to feel like they were in Napa, with a Shakespearean touch to honor the arts focus for the evening." Sheril chose natural pieces, including wooden wine barrels, Tuscan-style chairs, rustic wooden chargers and a multitude of candles, which were a nod to Shakespeare's candlelit Globe Theatre. A hallmark of her design for the evening was the place card holders: wine corks from Cornerstone and Stepping Stone bottles, of course.

The night began with wine and cocktails in the living room and kitchen, giving guests the chance to interact with chefs Jackson Kramer and Nick Seabergh. An alluring announcement drew guests away from the bustling pace in the kitchen as Dan McCleary and Stephanie Shine, the husband-and-wife duo at the helm of the Tennessee Shakespeare Company, invited guests outside for a moonlit performance. Beni and Mike's pool area with seating on the steps served as an outdoor amphitheatre, allowing guests to see Shakespeare performed in a picturesque and playful setting. Dan and Stephanie performed Shakespearean highlights, including his musings on food, wine and love. As Beni observed, "You couldn't help but be a fan of Tennessee Shakespeare. They were so much fun and brought their own energy to the party. The way they performed was so appropriate for the night."

Shakespeare set the stage for the meal: a multi-course, wine-filled performance in itself. Mike and Beni never dictate the menu on occasions like this one, saying, "We tell the chefs 'You guys come up with the menu and we'll match the wine.' We've had absolutely inspired meals. They're able to cook what's fresh and cook what they're inspired by at that time." Mike simply requests that the menu consist of several smaller courses because he enjoys the opportunity to try many different dishes, and, of course, select more wines for pairing.

JACKSON KRAMER

JACKSON KRAMER is a native Memphian who began his career at The Grove Grill. After attending the Western Culinary Institute in Portland, Oregon, he worked as a private chef and at restaurants across the country, including the Richmond Hill Inn in Asheville, North Carolina. He was the head chef at Interim Restaurant from 2007 until 2009 and from 2011 until 2014. He will open Broad Avenue's first farm to table restaurant, Bounty on Broad in the fall, 2014.

NICK SEABERGH

A Vicksburg, Mississippi, native, NICK SEABERGH studied the culinary arts at Delgado College in New Orleans and MUW in Columbus, Mississippi. He has worked as the Executive Chef of the Giardiana's at the Alluvian Hotel in Greenwood, Mississippi and at Alchemy Memphis.

L to r: Chefs Jackson Kramer, Nick Seabergh

L to r: Chefs Jackson Kramer, Nick Seabergh, Walt Stallings

"The biggest thing was the wine. We knew we had a lot of wine so we needed a lot of courses."
–Jackson Kramer

"When we host dinners we ask the chefs to cook what they're inspired by at the time. Anything they come up with, we will have a wine to match."
–Beni Dragutsky

Chef Jackson Kramer and host, Beni Dragutsky

Mike says he'd rather eat nine small courses because you get to pair more wine that way.
L to r: Bobby Weekly, Lisa Franklin, Beni and Mike Dragutsky

The Dragutsky wine cellar, stunning the senses. L to r: Carrie McPeters, Bobby Weekly, Chef Jackson Kramer, Lisa Franklin

Jackson and Nick took Mike's request for smaller dishes to heart, serving up nine courses throughout the evening. While it may seem like an arduous task, Nick remembers that to plan the menu he and Jackson simply "had some beers at the deli and came up with the menu. I think that we wrote it on a bev nap." As Jackson explains their process, "Our styles were really similar, so it was easy to pick the food. It was autumn. The biggest thing was the wine. We knew he had a lot of wine, so we needed a lot of food."

After each of their courses, Nick and Jackson gave tableside talks about the dishes. Beni explains that the chefs interacting with guests is an important part of entertaining. "We do that every time we have a dinner," she says. "That's such an important part of the meal. You get to hear what they were thinking and it's a lot of fun. And they get to interact." Nick emphasizes that "the menu really showcased the wine. We initially wrote down proteins and it evolved from there."

It would be impossible to tell the story of Napa Chic without the story of Cornerstone and Stepping Stone wineries. A practicing physician by day, Mike is also an owner of two nationally acclaimed wineries. In the 1990s he and his medical partner David Sloas started nurturing their passions for wine, eventually becoming friends with cult Napa winemaker Randy Dunn. Mike recounts, "David was having lunch with Randy who mentioned that he had five extra tons of grapes. David called me and said 'Do you want to buy five tons of grapes?' I was just starting to learn about wine and we knew that these grapes made wine that was some of the most outstanding in Napa Valley. We knew a wine maker out there, and we started from scratch by coming up with a name in 1991. It was a right-place, right-time sort of thing."

> "We got involved with supporting the arts through wine. There is a social and giving spirit with wine that crosses over to the arts."
> –Mike Dragutsky

The winemaking process is totally under their control, from sourcing the grapes from farmers to the end product. During their first year they produced 300 cases and received one of the top reviews in the cabernet issue of *Wine Spectator*. In 2008, the winemakers brought Cornerstone to the next level. "We were a critically acclaimed winery, but with a small production," Mike says. "Then in 2008 the recession hit and many grapes became available in Napa because other wineries were cutting back. We decided to take the plunge and take it to the next level. Instead of making 1,000 cases of cabernet, we decided to increase our production ten plus

fold and not just cabernet, but also white wines and other grapes in all price ranges. We came from just cabernet to a winery that produces acclaimed wines on a wide spectrum."

Today they have a sister label, Stepping Stone Cellars, allowing them to produce $18 to $125 bottles of wine. They have also expanded to Oregon, working with one of the premier winemakers for pinot and chardonnay. Mike explains, "Today we have a tasting room in Napa, so we have a home. To do this was a five-year expansion. We got several people, mainly Memphians who love wine, to be brand ambassadors and partners in Cornerstone—Memphis' own winery."

While Cornerstone and Stepping Stone produce wines across the spectrum, when Beni and Mike were preparing for Napa Chic, there was one missing piece: a dessert wine. They were sitting outside of Great Wines & Spirits having lunch with a copy of *What to Drink with What You Eat*, the Bible of wine-pairing books, when Great Wines owner Gary Burhop happened by. Not only did he have a recommendation, he followed it up with a generous donation of two bottles of Le Tertre Du Lys D'Or, a 2005 Sauternes, for the party. Beni sees this random act of generosity as reflective of "how people in Memphis give."

As a transplant from Chicago, Beni originally was not sure how easy it would be to fully integrate herself into a smaller, Southern city. However, after she arrived, she came to realize that this transition was not going to be a difficult one. "Memphis has so much going for it," she says. "I don't think that Memphians realize just what an amazing city it is with the arts, chef-owned restaurants and everything that goes on here. It's also got to be one of the most philanthropic places to live. There are so many good-hearted people here who really put themselves out for all of these different organizations, making it a truly wonderful place to live. Memphis is one of these warm-hearted places; it's one in a million. For everyone in Memphis who thinks that the grass is greener, take it from someone who has lived in other places, *it isn't*."

The Dragutsky style of hosting with a purpose and the abundance of giving by the Napa Chic team underscores Memphis' legacy of commitment to its artistic and cultural assets and embodies the immortal words of William Shakespeare, "Good wine is a good familiar creature, if it be well used."

Stylist, Sheril Greenstein set the mood and the ambience with keen attention to detail.

Wooden chargers, Stepping Stone wine cork place card holders.

L to r: John Scharff, Chef Jackson Kramer

Local portrait artist, Kate Bradley captured guests with sketches, the ultimate party favor.
L to r: Dianne Jalfon, Ken Steinberg, Kate Bradley

The Tennessee Shakespeare Company brought their own energy to the party. Stephanie Shine, resident actor and education director

Dan McCleary, Founder and Producing Director is a native Memphian and graduate of Germantown High School.

Stephanie Shine gets Rabbi Micah Greenstein in the act.

Host Mike Dragutsky introduces each of his guests individually. As described by one guest, "a nice touch".

L to r: Merilyn Mangum, Richard Aycock, Claudia Moise, Mike Dragutsky, Beni Dragutsky, Ken Steinberg, Jill Steinberg

Smoked quail with chanterelles, pork belly, watercress and butternut squash.

"We had some beers at the deli and came up with the menu. I think we wrote it on a bev nap."
–Nick Seabergh

Sheril Greenstein wanted the guests to have a sweet remembrance, the sugar coated grapes. (Dip in egg whites and roll them in sugar.)

ArtsMemphis®
NAPA CHIC DINNER
FEATURING

CHEF JACKSON KRAMER OF   &   CHEF NICK SEABERGH OF
INTERIM RESTAURANT AND BAR   ALCHEMY MEMPHIS

WINE BY CORNERSTONE WINERIES
PROVIDED BY BENI AND MIKE DRAGUTSKY

APERITIF WINES
2010 STEPPING STONE RED ROCKS
2012 STEPPING STONE WHITE ROCKS

COURSE ONE
AMUSE BOUCHE
DUCK LIVER PATÉ, PEACH-GINGER GELÉE, CORNBREAD CROSTINI

COURSE TWO
SEARED DIVER SCALLOP, CREAMED CORN,
BLACKBERRY, CRISPY HAM, & SAGE
2012 STEPPING STONE PINOT GRIS
2010 CORNERSTONE SAUVIGNON BLANC

COURSE THREE
SMOKED QUAIL WITH CHANTERELLES, PORK BELLY,
WATERCRESS, & BUTTERNUT SQUASH
2010 STEPPING STONE SYRAH
2010 STEPPING STONE CABERNET FRANC

COURSE FOUR
"BELLY 'N BISCUIT"
PORK BELLY CONFIT, REDEYE GRAVY,
QUAIL EGG, & BUTTERMILK BISCUIT
2012 STEPPING STONE CORALLINA ROSÉ
2010 STEPPING STONE PINOT NOIR

COURSE FIVE
KING SALMON WITH FARRO, BRUSSELS, TARRAGON, & CIDER
2010 CORNERSTONE CHARDONNAY
2010 CORNERSTONE PINOT NOIR

COURSE SIX
TART APPLE SORBET WITH CANDIED GINGER

COURSE SEVEN
BOURBON-MISO GLAZED LAMB CHOP,
RED CURRY SWEET POTATO,
PISTACHIO MINT PESTO, & PICKLED ORANGE
2009 CORNERSTONE NAPA VALLEY CABERNET SAUVIGNON
2009 CORNERSTONE HOWELL MOUNTAIN
CABERNET SAUVIGNON

COURSE EIGHT
SWEETGRASS DAIRY CHEESES
(ASHER BLUE, THOMASVILLE THOME, AND GREENHILL)
WITH WILD PLUM, QUINCE & PEAR
2010 LA FLEUR D'OR SAUTERNES

COURSE NINE
CREME FRAICHE PANNA COTTA
KUMQUAT GELÉE & PECAN SHORTBREAD

L to r: Robert Hanusovsky, Merilyn Mangum, Richard Aycock

L to r: Cathy Helms, Don Helms, Marty Kelman

L to r: Pam Hauber, Steve West, Susan Thorpe

A pleased chef, Jackson Kramer

Sheril's nod to Napa, lots of candles and lanterns from the Garden District.

Delicate touch required for the quail eggs.

Pork belly confit, fried quail egg, red-eyed gravy and buttermilk biscuits.

According to Chef Nick Seabergh, working in the kitchen together was organic.

Crème fraîche panna cotta and pecan shortbread

Cheers Chef! L to r: Chef Jackson Kramer, stylist and guest,
Sheril Greenstein, Mike Dragutsky, Micah Greenstein, Richard Scharff

Mike Dragutsky, Micah Greenstein

L to r: Daniel Weickenand, and wife Dianne Jalfon,
Brent Addington, Susan Thorpe, Chef Jackson Kramer

The guests cheered, "Long live ArtsMemphis!" guest, Don Helms

PORK BELLY CONFIT, FRIED QUAIL EGG, RED-EYED GRAVY AND BUTTERMILK BISCUITS

NICK SEABERGH

PORK BELLY CONFIT:

- 2 TABLESPOONS KOSHER SALT
- 4 TABLESPOONS BROWN SUGAR
- ¼ CUP BOURBON
- 2 SPRIGS ROSEMARY, REMOVED FROM STEM
- 2 BAY LEAVES, CRUSHED
- 1 TABLESPOON BLACK PEPPERCORNS
- 1 TABLESPOON CRUSHED RED PEPPER
- ¼ TEASPOON CURING SALT
- 1 (5 POUND) PORK BELLY, SKIN ON
- ENOUGH PORK FAT, OR DUCK FAT TO COVER THE PORK BELLY

Make a course paste out of the first 8 ingredients and rub generously all over pork belly. Place pork belly in a plastic bag and refrigerate 12 hours or overnight to cure.

Remove pork belly from the cure, rinse and pat dry. Place pork belly in a pan, with a rack that will fit it snuggly.

Heat duck or pork fat in a pan to about 200 degrees then pour over pork belly. Cover with a lid and confit the belly at 225 degrees for about 4 hours or until a butter knife will twist easily when placed in the pork.

Remove pork belly from the oven and allow to cool to almost room temperature but still warm.

Carefully remove the pork belly from the fat, reserve the tasty fat for another use.

Place pork belly skin side down between two pans lined with parchment paper and place a 3½ pound weight on top of it and refrigerate until it is completely cooled (this will give the belly a nice uniform shape). Once pork belly is cooled, it can be sliced into 4 ounce uniform slices.

RED-EYED GRAVY:

- 7 OUNCES FATTY HAM SCRAPS
- 2 QUARTS SMOKY PORK STOCK MADE FROM HAM HOCKS OR SMOKED NECKBONES AND MIREPOIX
- ¼ CUP "PEANUT BUTTER" COLORED ROUX
- 1 CUP FRESHLY BREWED GOOD, BLACK COFFEE
- 2 SPRIGS FRESH THYME

In a cast iron Dutch oven, fry the ham scraps over medium-high heat until they render some fat and begin to develop a fond on the bottom of the pan, the whole while scraping the fond from the bottom of the pan.

Deglaze with 2 ounces of the stock and reduce until another fond forms. Repeat this 3 times then add the remaining stock and bring to a boil. When the stock has reached a boil, add cooled roux and reduce to slightly thicker than sauce consistency.

Add coffee, thyme and a little black pepper. Allow thyme and ham to steep in the gravy.

Strain the gravy to remove the ham and thyme. Skim any fat that may have collected on the surface.

Check seasoning, the ham should be salty enough to sufficiently season the gravy. Keep warm.

BISCUITS:

- 12 CUPS SELF-RISING SOUTHERN-STYLE FLOUR (WHITE LILY® BRAND)
- 4 TABLESPOONS SUGAR
- 4 TABLESPOONS PLUS 2 TEASPOONS SALT
- 1 TEASPOON BAKING SODA
- 1 POUND VERY COLD LARD
- ½ GALLON BUTTERMILK
- 2 CUPS HEAVY CREAM
- 8 CUPS ALL-PURPOSE FLOUR
- BUTTER, MELTED, FOR BRUSHING TOPS

Sift all dry ingredients into a large bowl.

Using your fingers, cut in the lard until flour resembles small pebbles. Add buttermilk and cream; stir until the mixture just comes together and resembles the texture of thick cottage cheese. Let rest in the refrigerator for 20 minutes.

Place flour in a large bowl. Drop 2 ounces of dough at a time into flour and form into little balls. Arrange them uniformly on a sheet pan lined with parchment paper and nonstick cooking spray.

Bake at 425 degrees for 12 minutes or until the tops are golden brown. Remove from the oven and brush generously with melted butter.

TO ASSEMBLE:

On a griddle or large cast iron skillet, gently crisp the pork belly pieces in bacon fat. Place, open faced, on a split biscuit. Over very low heat in the same pan, very gently fry quail eggs in bacon fat. Sauce biscuit with gravy and add fried egg with some chopped chives and eat.

SMOKED QUAIL

JACKSON KRAMER

- 4 SEMI-BONELESS QUAIL
- KOSHER SALT
- 1 LARGE BUTTERNUT SQUASH
- 2 TABLESPOONS CREAM
- 1 TABLESPOON HONEY
- 6 OUNCES FRESH CHANTERELLE MUSHROOMS, CLEANED
- 1 TABLESPOON BUTTER
- 4 OUNCES WATERCRESS, CLEANED
- 4 OUNCES ROASTED PORK BELLY, LARGE DICED

For quail, clip the wings and season with kosher salt. Let them sit out at room temperature for 1 hour while you get the smoker ready. Once the smoker is ready (I used cherry wood) place the quail in until lightly smoked and cooked to medium. Remove from smoker and keep warm.

For butternut squash, preheat the oven to 400 degrees. Cut squash in half and roast cut side down for 45 minutes. Let it cool, and then scoop out the insides into a food processor. Add cream, honey, and a pinch of salt. Puree until smooth.

For mushrooms, sauté them for a few minutes in butter. Once soft add watercress and pork belly. Cook for another few minutes until watercress is wilted.

To plate, smear a nice spoonful of the squash purée on a plate and add some of the mushroom/watercress on top. Take off the legs of the quail and place the breast down first on top of the mushroom/watercress and then crisscross the legs on top of the breast.

SEARED DIVER SCALLOP, CREAMED CORN, BLACKBERRY, CRISPY HAM AND SAGE

NICK SEABERGH

HAM AND SAGE:

- 6 PIECES VERY THINLY SLICED, UNCOOKED AGED COUNTRY HAM (BENTON'S 14 MONTH OLD IS GOOD HERE)
- HANDFUL OF PICKED SAGE LEAVES TOSSED IN OLIVE OIL

Preheat oven to 350 degrees.

On a sheet pan with a rack, lay ham slices flat over the rack. Sprinkle with sage leaves. Turn the oven off; place ham and sage inside. Leave in oven overnight. Remove from oven next day. Ham and sage should be very crispy but not at all browned. Set aside until ready to plate.

CREAMED CORN:

- 12 EARS SWEET CORN
- ½ OF A SMALL ONION, FINELY DICED
- 4 TABLESPOONS WHOLE BUTTER, DIVIDED
- PINCH OF CAYENNE
- SALT, TO TASTE
- 2 CUPS HALF-AND-HALF
- FINELY SLICED GREEN ONION

Remove corn kernels from the cob using a knife, set half aside and keep the cobs. Using the back of a knife, scrape the "milk" from the cobs into a blender.

Sweat onion over low heat in half the butter until it becomes sweet and translucent. Add half of the corn and cayenne; season with salt. Cook until corn is sweet and just done. Add corn mixture to the blender with half-and half; purée until very smooth.

Slightly brown remaining half of the corn and green onion in remaining half of the butter. Add the purée and heat through; hold until ready to plate.

BLACKBERRY GASTRIQUE:

- 1 CUP WHITE GRANULATED SUGAR
- ½ CUP WHITE WINE VINEGAR
- ½ CUP FRESHLY SQUEEZED ORANGE JUICE
- 4 CUPS BLACKBERRIES

Over medium heat in a slope-sided 2 quart saucepan, heat sugar until it becomes liquid and slightly light reddish brown.

Add liquids and blackberries. Cook over low heat until reduced to sauce consistency. Sugar should be dissolved and blackberries disintegrated. Pass through a fine mesh strainer. Hold warm until plating.

SCALLOPS:

- 6 SCALLOPS
- SALT AND PEPPER
- 1 OUNCE CLARIFIED BUTTER
- SALT AND WHITE PEPPER

Pat scallops dry and season with salt and pepper. Heat clarified butter in a skillet until steaming hot and beginning to smoke. Add scallops to the pan and brown on each side (do not move scallops other than to turn them over into a different location in the pan from where the previous side had cooked).

TO ASSEMBLE:

Place some creamed corn on a plate and top with scallops, drizzle blackberry gastrique around and garnish with ham crisps and sage.

SAVORY SOUTH

A TRULY DISTINCT STYLE IS A RARE AND HARD QUALITY TO COME BY, but Nancy McNamee accomplished just that with her inspiriting of Savory South, the Culinary Series dinner she hosted. On a warm November evening, guests of all ages gathered in Nancy's home to enjoy the high class cuisine of legendary Memphis chef Erling Jensen and the power of prose with an uproariously irreverent performance by local theatre company, Voices of the South.

Upon arrival guests were greeted with the sophisticated hospitality embodied by their hostess. While they sipped champagne and enjoyed lively conversation, attendees were also treated to an intimate and unfettered look inside a truly spectacular home. Decorated in her distinct, signature style, Nancy's home includes treasures from around the world. Mirrors and sleek edges provide a modern touch, while Asian art and artifacts lend an exotic, international flair. Carefully curated artwork and one-of-a-kind design elements evoke the elegance and craftsmanship that Nancy seeks relentlessly and shares selflessly.

There was no debate as to who would style Savory South: Greg Campbell. Greg, owner of the local floral shop Garden District, is a master of inventive and spectacular floral designs, and event styling. He has worked with Nancy and has been a close personal friend for over a decade. "I don't remember a time when I didn't know Greg Campbell," Nancy says. As a result of their long history of working together, they knew exactly how they wanted the party to look. As Nancy recounts, "We decided on black and white because that's a reflection of who I am." Greg adds, "We made the party look like Nancy."

The evening flowed from cocktails in the living room to dinner on the terrace. So that guests could take in the beauty of the night and the sparkling pool, Nancy and Greg opted for a dramatic clear tent. Greg recalls the decision, "We went with beautiful black and white, and then we decided to do the clear tent on the terrace. We had done a tent there before, but not a clear one. It got a little warm, but once the sun went away, it was perfect."

While Nancy's home remained perfectly tranquil throughout the night, the fully equipped catering kitchen was a hub of activity. Because she entertains so often, Nancy's garage also doubles as a kitchen. Of course, it is artfully decorated with sculptures by her nephew, renowned artist Randall Andrews. Randall, who recently moved from Los Angeles back to his hometown, Clarksdale, Mississippi, is best known for his found objects installations that span the country. She explains, "He does wall sculptures as well as smaller pieces. I called him and said, 'We've got to make my garage into a caterer's kitchen because my real kitchen's in the middle of things.' But I couldn't have it look unsightly. I told him that I wanted it to be metal and he brought the pieces. It's a combination of auto parts and stainless cookware."

The cleverly appointed drive-in kitchen was a great space for Erling to work his magic. His meal included clams and quail and wowed guests with its flavor and presentation. He recounts that the ideas behind the dinner came from Nancy herself. "I went over to Nancy's and met with her. We talked about her likes and dislikes, and that's what inspired me for the meal."

ERLING JENSEN

ERLING JENSEN is the Executive Chef and owner of Erling Jensen. A native of Denmark, Erling began his culinary career in the United States as the chef at the Danish Embassy in Washington, D.C. After working in Miami, he moved to Memphis to work at La Tourelle in 1989. After seven years there and numerous accolades, he opened his eponymous restaurant in 1996, which was named "Best Restaurant in Memphis" for ten consecutive years. Erling has cooked at the James Beard House twice and has been featured in numerous publications including *Southern Living and Food and Wine*.

L to r: Estella, Delorise, Chef Erling Jensen

Erling's meal came together elegantly and represents his style of refined, timeless cuisine. Though his restaurant, Erling Jensen, has been in existence since 1996, it has stayed current, and Erling is enthusiastic about the local food scene in Memphis. "Right now it's just blooming. I think people are going out to eat more and more. What I'd like to see are more local restaurants: Eat local. Buy local. We buy everything as local as we can. Now everyone can buy local because there are more local farmers than there were ten or fifteen years ago. Today, farmers approach the restaurant and just knock on the door."

Dinner was served on Nancy's own tableware, enhanced by the optic crystal obelisks by specialty designer, Veritas Glass. The interplay between the unique crystal stemware and the lighting from the table and the pool, created a dramatic, warm effect. After dinner, Erling treated guests to a talk about the meal that was chock-full of his signature sense of humor.

Stylist, Greg Campbell working his magic.

Voices of the South may conjure up the notion of singers, but this unique Memphis theatre troupe celebrates distinctive voices in writing as they create, produce and perform theatre from diverse Southern perspectives. After the meal, company members Alice Berry and Jenny Odle Madden performed their original adaptation of Eudora Welty's short story "Why I Live at the P.O." Amid an audience of dinner guests and with a lone prop, the star performers executed the high-spirited scene with brilliant use of body language and facial expression. They conveyed the quirky humor of Welty and the pure pleasure of her prose. As Jenny explains of Voices of the South's work, "When we first started, our hope with the southern short story adaptations is that they would make audiences want to read more literature." Judging by the rapt postures and loud laughs, guests certainly will be reading more Eudora Welty.

The evening ended with a full moon and Nancy's serene Buddha statues keeping watch over the party from across the pool. And though Savory South eventually came to an end, with younger guests lingering into the night, the party setup and spirit came to life again the next day when Nancy decided to invite friends over for a backyard Savory South Redux. "The next night everything was still up, so we went to Corky's and got barbeque and had fifteen or eighteen

The artistic and palate pleasing drive-in kitchen designed by sculptor, Randall Andrews.

of us who sat at the still elegantly adorned tables. We had barbeque, coleslaw and baked beans." While pickup barbeque may be slightly different from the quail that Erling served, this moment shows everything that is Savory about the South and the extent to which Nancy and her friends are a good natured, good time-loving group.

Guests and tables glow in the reflection of Nancy's collectable crystal.

Anthony Logan, server

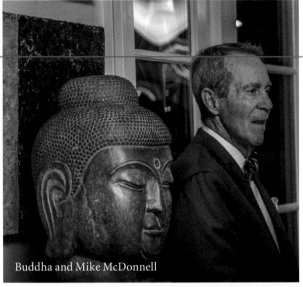

Buddha and Mike McDonnell

Asian inspired décor and mirrors create a dramatic, yet soothing effect. L to r: Barbara Sysak, Gary Sysak, Gail George, Nancy Willis, Lane Moten

The Buddhas bestowing good fortune upon the party guests.

L to r: Ray George, Anthony Logan, Steve West

Clear tent on the terrace, a first.

L to r: Jeff McEvoy, Barbara Sysak, Emily McEvoy, Courtenay McAllister, Tom McAllister, Gary Sysak

L to r: Jana Tayloe, McNeal McDonnell

"The evening ended with a full moon and Nancy's serene Buddha statues keeping watch over the party from across the pool. And though the Savory South party eventually concluded, with younger guests lingering into the night, the party setup and spirit came to life again the next day when Nancy decided to invite friends over for a backyard Savory South Redux.

L to r: Nancy McNamee, Greg Campbell, Erling Jensen

L to r: Margaret McLean, Tom McAllister, Susan Schadt, Pamela Hauber, Greg Campbell, Linda Shea, Tom Miller

L to r: Mary Jo Miller, Trip Tayloe, Bickie McDonnell

Final touches. Erling Jensen

The beauty of fine art emulated by the grace of Ginori china.

L to r: Gary Sysak, Elise Lake, Alec McLean

The sweet side of art.

L to r: Nancy Thomas, Jana Tayloe, Gary Sysak

Erling takes a bow. L to r: Mike McDonnell, Emily McEvoy, Erling Jensen, Margaret McLean, Susan Schadt, Tom McAllister

Voices of the South Actors Alice Rainey-Berry, Jenny Odle Madden. Bickie McDonnell, Nancy Willis, Chuck Schadt

Nancy McNamee, Pam McDonnell, Mike McDonnell

Pamela Hauber, Greg Campbell

Alice Rainey-Berry, Jenny Odle Madden perform Eudora Welty's "Why I Live at the P.O."

Jenny Odle Madden, Alice Rainey-Berry

RACK OF LAMB WITH MASHED SWEET POTATOES

ERLING JENSEN

Serves 4

- 1½ POUNDS OF AUSTRALIAN RACK OF LAMB

MARINADE:

- 1 CUP MOLASSES
- ½ CUP CHOPPED GARLIC
- ½ CUP DIJON MUSTARD
- ½ CUP WHOLE GRAIN MUSTARD

Mix marinade ingredients together. Place cleaned lamb in marinade for 12 hours. Take lamb out and remove some of the marinade from lamb. Put in a 450 degree oven for 10 minutes. Turn the oven down to 300 degrees and bake it until desired degree of doneness.

MASHED SWEET POTATOES:

- 2-3 LARGE SWEET POTATOES
- ¼ CUP HONEY
- ¼ CUP LIGHT BROWN SUGAR
- 3 OUNCES CHOPPED BRAZIL NUTS
- SALT AND PEPPER, TO TASTE

Cut sweet potatoes in half. Place on a baking sheet and place in a 350 degree oven for 45 minutes.

Scrape out the insides and mix with honey, light brown sugar, Brazil nuts, salt and pepper to taste.

QUAIL STUFFED WITH BISON MEAT AND TRUFFLES

ERLING JENSEN

SERVES 4

- ½ POUND GROUND BISON MEAT
- 2 TEASPOONS TRUFFLE OIL
- 1 TEASPOON TRUFFLE SLICES
- 4 SEMI-BONELESS QUAILS (FROZEN OR FRESH)
- ⅓ CUP HEAVY CREAM
- SALT AND PEPPER, TO TASTE
- 2 EGGS

Mix bison meat with truffle oil, truffle slices, heavy cream, salt and pepper to taste. Stuff the quail with bison mixture, using a pastry bag or spoon. Bake in the oven for about 12 minutes at 375 degrees.

SING FOR YO SUPPA

MEMPHIS IS FAMOUS FOR HAVING SACRED GROUND SITES, Memphis milestones not found anywhere else in the world: Sun Studios, Stax, Graceland and the National Civil Rights Museum immediately come to mind. The Metal Museum occupies its own sacred ground and distinctive position in the museum world, both displaying and making art. This stunningly beautiful site, overlooking the imposing Mississippi River, forged camaraderie and community providing the spirited aura that defined High Cotton Soul-Table/Sing for Yo Suppa.

Memphis chef, restaurateur and entrepreneur Karen Carrier and her guest chefs Derek Emerson, chef-owner of Walkers Drive In and Local 463 in Jackson, Mississippi, and Bret "Shaggy" Duffee, Chef de Cuisine of Bayona in New Orleans, forged their culinary and artistic talents atop the bluffs of the Mississippi River, amidst the museum's handsome historic buildings, shady oaks and funky metal sculptures to fire up High Cotton Soul-Table/Sing for Yo Suppa.

One of Memphis' hidden gems, the Metal Museum is the only facility in the country dedicated to the promotion and preservation of metalworking. Founded in 1976, the museum occupies the buildings of a former United States Merchant Marine hospital in the French Fort neighborhood, located just minutes from Downtown Memphis. Today the museum consists of a main gallery building, the library, which contains 6,000 books and portfolios on metalwork, the Lawler Foundry, the Schering-Plough Smithy and residences for blacksmith apprentices. It is a national center for metal arts, attracting visitors, supporters and metal workers from around the country.

"The icing on the cake was pie," freshly baked by –Chef Emma Lincoln

Metal Museum Executive Director Carissa Hussong explains that, "The Museum presents some of the finest metalwork ever created, educates future master metalsmiths and provides hands-on experiences for aspiring young artists and future patrons. With sparks flying in the smithy, molten metal in the foundry, elegant sculpture in the gardens and a wide selection of finely crafted metalwork in the galleries, there is something to delight even the most discerning visitor."

Guests were greeted by museum employees just inside the 10th Anniversary Museum Gates adorned with doorknob size metal rosettes made by metalsmiths from around the world. The guests stopped to scan the whimsical and personal Anniversary Gates and the fabulous assemblage of mounted artists statements prior to touring the main gallery and the Museum's Mobile Forge for an on-site blacksmith demonstration.

The spectacle of the setting was highlighted by chef Karen Carrier's eclectic taste in all things culinary, and her notorious daring décor. The evening was bound to be full of surprises in palate and place. Gasps were audible as guests turned the corner and were struck by the dramatic sight of one long table, set for eighty, placed perpendicular to the river. The tables were set with several four-foot tall sculptures by Wayne Edge, a distinctive local artist and personal friend of Karen's, and lights were strung up above. The moon, the Mississippi River and mojitos were thrown in to boot!

KAREN CARRIER

KAREN BLOCKMAN CARRIER returned from New York City to Memphis in 1987 and launched a catering company, Another Roadside Attraction Catering. In 1991, she opened Automatic Slim's Tonga Club, a sibling to the original outpost in New York. Having sold Memphis' Automatic Slim's in 2008, Karen's eateries now include Beauty Shop Restaurant and Lounge, which was included in *Gourmet's* "America's Top 100 Restaurants" in 2002 and Conde Nast Traveler's "Hot Tables" in 2003. In addition, she owns Bar DKDC and Mollie Fontaine Lounge. In 2011, CNN highlighted Karen as a successful restaurateur and small business owner. Karen was invited to cook for the prestigious James Beard House in New York City in 2000 and again in 2006. She is also a featured chef in *Wild Abundance: Ritual, Revelry & Recipes of the South's Finest Hunting Clubs.*

BRETT "SHAGGY" DUFFEE

BRETT DUFFEE was born and raised on the Westbank in New Orleans. He has worked at Tsunami, Felicia Suzanne's, The Beauty Shop, Do Sushi and Equestria in Memphis. He is currently the Chef de Cuisine at Bayona in New Orleans. A self-taught chef, Brett's style of cooking is based on sustainable agriculture and the Deep South food traditions he grew up on.

DEREK EMERSON

DEREK EMERSON, Executive Chef and owner of Walker's Drive-In and Local 463 Urban Kitchen, has elevated the restaurant scene in Jackson, Mississippi. Both restaurants have received numerous local awards and accolades from such prestigious publications as *The New York Times, Southern Living, Mississippi Magazine* and *Continental Magazine*. He is also a featured chef in *Wild Abundance*. Derek was selected as a semifinalist for "Best Chef: South in the 2008, 2009 and 2010" James Beard Foundation Awards and has served on the Atlanta Food and Wine Festival Advisory Council.

EMMA LINCOLN

EMMA LINCOLN is the owner of Emma Lincoln Catering, a full-service catering business in Memphis that serves "from two to 2,000." The catering business is a continuation of the company that her mother, Beneva Mayweather, formed in 1973. Emma joined the business in the mid-1970s and worked alongside her mother, taking on more and more responsibility throughout the years. Prior to her career in catering, Emma graduated from the University of Tennessee and earned a master's of library science from the University of Memphis. She was a teacher for two and a half years before joining her mother's business and starting a family, which includes son Daniel Watson, who is marketing a mix of spices from Beneva's recipes, and daughter Rashana Lincoln, who works with Emma. She is also a featured chef in *Wild Abundance*.

Chef Derek Emerson

Chef Karen Carrier

Chef Shaggy Duffee

Chef Emma Lincoln

Karen was inspired when she participated in a rustic, yet refined, "Outstanding in the Field" dinner, where she reconnected with chef Derek Emerson after initially working with him at a New Orleans book launch for *Wild Abundance: Ritual, Revelry & Recipes of the South's Finest Hunting Clubs.* They enjoy working together so much that she recruited him to come to Memphis for the party. As Derek recounts, "She called and asked and I said 'Of course.' If she asked me to go to Minnesota and cook in a snowstorm, I'd say yes. I love Karen; her spirit is just so awesome. Her food's always great, and her attitude is always great. She's real straightforward." Karen also brought in New Orleans chef Brett "Shaggy" Duffee who worked for her in Memphis before moving to New Orleans. Prior to the dinner, Derek and Shaggy did not know each other but the end of the evening found them to be fast friends. "It's great to meet someone like Derek who you can hang out with and talk about food," says Shaggy.

"It brings back Southern roots of Sunday supper. Everyone would get together and make a connection with everybody else by passing the plates." –Derek Emerson

This spirit of easygoing camaraderie and community carried over to the dinner. Guests were seated communally and served family style. Explaining the genius in her design, Karen explains, "Family style gets people reaching across each other and communicating. You have to talk to the person next to you. By sharing food outside, it sends the message that this is not formal. This community goes right down the table. That was the whole point of doing a long table. It was sort of like giving grace and an act of love."

Guests shared Karen's unlikely pairing of watermelon salad and decadent mussels "tower" to start, and the buzz began. Shaggy followed suit with a dramatically plated braised branzino fish, a tongue-in-cheek take on trout amandine, inspired by Greek culinary traditions. Derek did not disappoint, but rather brought out with guns blazing, braised wagyu beef cheeks. Expounding on the family-style feel of the night, he says, "It brings back Southern roots of Sunday supper. Everyone would get together and make a connection with everybody else by passing the plates. Tonight people from different parts of the city are meeting each other by passing around the food. When you've got eighty people at a table, you've got to talk to everyone. It was amazing how the meal worked with the art and the sun going down. It's hard to duplicate something like that. It was just beautiful."

The "icing on the cake" was pies! Memphis chef Emma Lincoln, owner of Emma Mayweather Lincoln, caterer and co-author of *Our Mother's Table: The Culinary Journey of Beneva Mayweather,* baked her mother's famous decades old recipes for chocolate and blueberry pies. The coveted confections were shared up and down the common table with the requisite nudging and a few audible "a-hems" recognizable at all family dinners.

The beauty and the beat of the entertainment for the evening was music by soulful swamp princess Marcella Simien & Her Lovers. She had a very special guest straight from the Bayou: two-time Grammy-award winning zydeco artist and her father, Terrence Simien. A Lafayette, Louisiana, native, Marcella Simien moved to Memphis to attend the Memphis College of Art in 2009. She has established a musical following in Memphis, playing weekly at two of Karen's establishments, Mollie Fontaine Lounge and Bar DKDC.

Remembering the evening, Marcella says, "The Metal Museum's location atop that Mississippi River bluff is absolutely perfect for an event that celebrates Southern culture. Standing high up there, you can feel the history in the wind, can feel it seep into your skin. That we gathered on the banks of the river was a nod to this, and reiterated the undeniable cultural connection these states share. Having chefs from New Orleans, Jackson and Memphis was absolutely perfect, and the meal was a masterpiece in itself. Being able to help set the tone with the music was truly an honor for my band and me. Having my mother and father present was the cherry on top."

The soul-stirring, foot-stomping zydeco sounds got guests on their feet and responding resonantly to Karen's call, "So get up, get out, get ready to move, shift, push, let yo' backbone slip and stomp yo' feet. Be here — nuff said!"

The calm before the storm, server's jacket at the ready.

Selfie on the bluff. L to r: Stevann Lazich, Shaggy Duffy

Josh Muller carries the weight.

Karen's vision. "The whole point of doing a long table was like giving grace and an act of love."

Wayne Edge sculpture in silhouette.

Wayne Edge sculpture detail.

L to r: Derek Emerson, Keith Rawlings, Karen Carrier

Shaggy Duffy, taste as you go.

Chefs fire it up. L to r: Stephanie Thomas, Karen Carrier, Shaggy Duffy, Derek Emerson

Karen called and asked Derek to come. "If she asked me to come to Minnesota and cook in a snowstorm I would say yes."
Left to right: Shaggy Duffy, Karen Carrier, and Derek Emerson.

Shaggy Duffy tends the fire.

Family style plating. L to r: Jenny Dempsey, Derek Emerson, Shay Widmer, Shaggy Duffy, Stephanie Thomas

Smithy Michael Chmielewski, demonstrates the Metal Museum's mobile forge.

"Seeing how the metal worked with the art and the sun going down was a unique experience. It's hard to duplicate something like that. It was just beautiful." –Derek Emerson

Stephanie Thomas

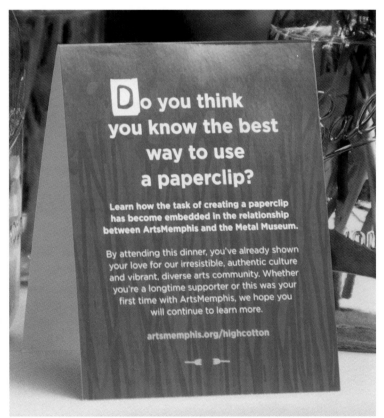

Do you think you know the best way to use a paperclip?

Learn how the task of creating a paperclip has become embedded in the relationship between ArtsMemphis and the Metal Museum.

By attending this dinner, you've already shown your love for our irresistible, authentic culture and vibrant, diverse arts community. Whether you're a longtime supporter or this was your first time with ArtsMemphis, we hope you will continue to learn more.

artsmemphis.org/highcotton

Marcella + Her Lovers sing for our suppa! L to r: Marcella Simien, Frank McLallen, Ben Bauermeister.

Chef Shaggy Duffy and his tongue and cheek nod to the heat, prepares a local Mediterranean favorite, Bronzino.

"I see a lot of young people going out to eat, it's a big part of their evening and they are willing to try different foods. There's an energy and a whole new way of looking at the dining experience that's happening now."
–Shaggy Duffy

L to r: Janet Seessel, Gary Wunderlich, Morgan Zanone, Philip Zanone.

Native Louisiana steppers, Lauren Boyer and Greg Baudoin.

Doug Ferris, Dot Neale, make the rounds.

Dave DePeters, Mary Lee Formanek, Peter Formanek, Charles Hubbert, Maggie Hubbert flanked by a Wayne Edge sculpture and the energy of Zydeco.

Dancing the night away. Greg Baudoin, Sheila Cullen.

Terrence Simien

Music by Marcella + Her Lovers: the Louisiana Soulful Swamp Princess and her amazing band with a very special guest straight from the Bayou: Grammy-award winning Zydeco artist Terrance Simien. "So get up, get out, get ready to move, shift, push, let yo' backbone slip and stomp yo' feet. Be here – nuff said!"
–Karen Carrier

L to r: Chris Golightly, Mayor Luttrell and his wife

L to r: Amy Howell, David Lusk and Carissa Hussong, Wayne Edge

Bill Craddock and daughter, Maysey.

Chef Shaggy Duffy and guest, Myron Mall

Karen's inspiration. "People in New Orleans are dying to live. I am trying to instill that in this city." L to r: Stephanie Thomas, Karen Carrier

BRAISED WAGYU BEEF CHEEKS

DEREK EMERSON

- 3 CUPS OIL
- 5 CUPS ALL-PURPOSE FLOUR
- 3 POUNDS CHEEKS (SILVER SKIN REMOVED)
- 1 BUNCH OF CELERY, ROUGHLY CHOPPED
- 1 BUNCH OF CARROTS, ROUGHLY CHOPPED
- 4 LARGE ONIONS, ROUGHLY CHOPPED
- 1 CUP CHOPPED GARLIC
- 1 CUP ORANGE ZEST
- 4 CUPS RED WINE
- 4 CUPS ORANGE JUICE
- 3 QUARTS VEAL STOCK
- ½ GALLON DICED TOMATOES
- 4 BAY LEAVES
- FRESH THYME AND ROSEMARY SPRIGS
- SALT AND PEPPER, TO TASTE

In a braising pan, add oil. Flour cheeks and brown on all the sides of the cheek pieces. As cheeks are browned, remove pieces to a holding pan.

Add celery, carrots, and onions; sauté about 10 minutes or until lightly caramelized, add garlic and orange zest. Deglaze braising pan with red wine and orange juice. Let the liquids reduce to half.

Add veal stock, tomatoes, bay leaves, thyme, rosemary, and pepper. Allow to simmer and reduce slightly. Nest cheek pieces in the top layer of the vegetable mixture. Stock should cover the cheeks; add more stock if needed. Salt to taste.

Contents should be covered and allowed to simmer for at least 20 minutes. Then braise in a 300 degree oven for 3½-4 hours or until knife tender.

When done, remove cheeks from braising liquid and set to the side. Strain liquid to remove vegetables, saving the dark rich sauce. Place cheeks back in sauce and hold in 200 degree oven until ready to serve.

ROASTED GARLIC

DEREK EMERSON

- 3 HEADS ELEPHANT GARLIC
- ¼ CUP OLIVE OIL
- SALT AND PEPPER, TO TASTE

Preheat oven to 425 degrees.

Peel away outer layers of garlic bulb skin, leaving skins of the individual cloves intact.

Place garlic on a piece of foil. Drizzle with olive oil and season with salt and pepper to taste. Wrap garlic tightly in a foil purse and place in an oven safe dish or on a baking sheet.

Bake until very tender, about 45 minutes or so.

When tender remove from oven, let cool, cut off top (end with the point), squeeze into a food processer and purée until smooth. Put in a container and save for later.

WHITE BEAN PURÉE

DEREK EMERSON

- 4 TABLESPOONS DUCK FAT OR BUTTER
- 1 LARGE ONION, DICED
- 1 TABLESPOON CHOPPED GARLIC
- 1 PINCH CAYENNE
- 4 CANS OR ABOUT 6 CUPS CANNELLINI BEANS
- 2-3 CUPS CHICKEN STOCK
- 1 TABLESPOON CHOPPED FRESH THYME
- SALT AND PEPPER, TO TASTE
- 2 BAY LEAVES

In a saucepan, melt duck fat or butter. Add onion, garlic, and cayenne; cook over moderate heat until tender.

Add beans, stock, thyme, salt and pepper and bay leaves; bring everything to a simmer then reduce heat to low. Cook until beans are really soft, about 20-30 minutes.

When soft, remove from heat and drain, reserve the liquid for adjusting the thickness of purée.

Remove bay leaves and place drained beans in a food processer. Start processing, adding liquid as needed until smooth and silky.

Add as much garlic mixture as you would like. Check seasoning and adjust with salt and pepper as needed.

You can keep warm in a low oven or double boiler until ready to use.

BRUSSELS SPROUTS AND CELERY ROOT CHIFFONADE

DEREK EMERSON

- 2 POUNDS BRUSSELS SPROUTS
- 1 HEAD CELERY ROOT
- 1 STICK BUTTER
- 1 TABLESPOON OLIVE OIL
- 2 WHOLE SHALLOTS, DICED SMALL
- 1 CUP CHICKEN STOCK
- 1 SPLASH SHERRY VINEGAR
- SALT AND PEPPER, TO TASTE

With a mandolin using the cutting blade, chiffonade all Brussels sprouts and set aside in a bowl for later sautéing.

Peel celery root. With a middle size cutting blade added to the mandolin, cut celery root. Should be the size of a matchstick. Add celery root to bowl with Brussels sprouts.

In a large sauté pan, melt and heat butter and olive oil; add shallots and sauté for 1 minute.

Add the celery root and Brussels sprouts mixture to sauté pan. Flip or toss on high until you start to get color then add chicken stock and cover for about 5 minutes or until everything is tender.

Right before serving give mixture a small shot of sherry vinegar for balance. Salt and pepper to taste.

FENNEL PEPPER CRUSTED BRANZINO, ESCAROLE "HORTA", BROWN BUTTER CAULIFLOWER JARDINÈRE

BRETT "SHAGGY" DUFFEE

BRANZINO:

- 4 WHOLE BRANZINO, SCALED AND GUTTED
- 1 CUP FENNEL PEPPER (¼ CUP GROUND FENNEL SEED, ¾ CUP COURSE GROUND BLACK PEPPER)
- DRY ROSEMARY BRANCHES SOAKED IN WATER
- EXTRA VIRGIN OLIVE OIL

Rinse fish and pat dry with paper towels. Rub fennel pepper into skin leaving a thick coat of spice on both sides. Refrigerate until ready to cook.

To Cook Fish: Once grill is heated, place soaked rosemary branches on top of flames creating an intoxicating aroma. Rub grill bars with olive oil and lightly place fish on surface. Do not move for 4-5 minutes. Flipping to the other side for another 3-4 minutes. Thermometer should read 140 degrees at the spine.

HORTA GREENS DRESSING:

- 2 CUPS EXTRA VIRGIN OLIVE OIL
- ZEST AND JUICE OF 2 LEMONS
- ½ CUP RED WINE VINEGAR
- 1 TABLESPOON MINCED GARLIC
- 1 TABLESPOON DRY OREGANO
- 1 CUP CHOPPED MINT
- 1 CUP CHOPPED PARSLEY
- 1 CUP CHOPPED DILL
- 1 RED ONION, THINLY SLICED

Place all dressing ingredients in a large mixing bowl whisk together. Set aside.

ESCAROLE HORTA:

- 1 HEAD ESCAROLE
- 1 BUNCH SPICY TURNIP GREENS OR MUSTARD GREENS
- SALT AND PEPPER, TO TASTE

Bring a large blanching pot of water up to boil; season with salt. In separate batches, blanch escarole and turnip or mustard greens until tender. Place both greens together in a colander to drain excess water. While still quite warm, squeeze as much water out as you can.

Cut greens into rather large chunks and place into horta dressing (recipe above) to marinade, adding salt and pepper to taste. Let marinate for a least 1 hour at room temperature.

BROWN BUTTER CAULIFLOWER JARDINÈRE

BROWN BUTTER CAULIFLOWER:

- 1 LARGE HEAD CAULIFLOWER, CUT INTO SMALL FLORETS
- 1 CUP UNSALTED BUTTER
- 5 ANCHOVY FILLETS
- ZEST AND JUICE OF 2 LEMONS
- SALT, TO TASTE

Toss florets with melted butter, anchovy fillets, lemon zest, lemon juice and salt.

Place in conventional oven at 375 degrees for 45 minutes, basting every 10 minutes until golden brown and cooked through.

FOR JARDINIÈRE...AKA PICKLES:

- 2 CUPS GOLDEN BALSAMIC VINEGAR
- 2 CUPS WATER
- 2 TABLESPOONS KOSHER SALT
- 1 TABLESPOON MUSTARD SEEDS
- 1 TEASPOON CHILE FLAKES
- 1 CUP SLICED GARLIC CLOVES
- 2 SLICES ORANGE ZEST
- 1 LARGE FENNEL BULB, LARGE DICED
- 1 LARGE OR 2 SMALL LEEKS CUT INTO SMALL DICE
- 1 CELERY STALK, LARGE DICE
- ½ TO ¾ CUP GOLDEN RAISINS
- ½ TO ¾ CUP MARCONA ALMONDS

Bring first 7 ingredients to a slow simmer and then toss in the fennel, leek and celery. Slowly cook vegetables in pickle solution until just al dente. Strain, reserving pickling juice for another application.

Toss pickled vegetables with browned cauliflower solution, and add golden raisins and marcona almonds. Leave at room temperature.

RAI RAM ROASTED LITTLENECK CLAMS/ MUSSELS AND SHRIMP IN OYSTER BUTTER BROTH WITH MANGO SHERRY PURÉE AND ARUGULA OIL

KAREN CARRIER

SERVES 4

- 2 TABLESPOONS OLIVE OIL
- 12 LITTLENECK CLAMS
- 16 MUSSELS
- ¾ CUP WHITE WINE
- 2 TABLESPOONS OYSTER SAUCE (THIS CAN BE PURCHASED AT AN ASIAN MARKET)
- 4 TABLESPOONS FLAT LEAF PARSLEY LEAVES
- 2 TABLESPOONS DICED ROASTED RED PEPPERS
- 1 HEAPING TABLESPOON MINCED GARLIC
- 3 TABLESPOONS UNSALTED BUTTER
- 8 GULF SHRIMP, PEELED AND DEVEINED WITH TAILS
- KOSHER SALT AND FRESHLY GROUND BLACK PEPPER, TO TASTE
- 1 BUNCH TORN RAI RAM (VIETNAMESE MINT) BUT REGULAR MINT WILL DO
- ½ BUNCH OF CILANTRO LEAVES, STEMS REMOVED

MANGO SHERRY SAUCE:

- 1-2 TABLESPOONS MANGO CHUTNEY
- ½ RIPE MANGO, PEELED
- ¼-½ CUP SHERRY

Put all ingredients in a blender until emulsified.

- ARUGULA OIL FOR DRIZZLING ON TOP

In a large skillet over medium high heat, add the olive oil. When the oil is hot add clams and sauté until you hear the clams start to pop releasing the clam liquor.

Add mussels, white wine, oyster sauce, parsley, roasted red pepper, garlic, and unsalted butter. Cover the skillet with a tight-fitting lid and steam the clams and mussels until they are completely opened. Discard any clams or mussels that do not open.

Once they are open, immediately add the shrimp. Season with salt and pepper to taste; remove from the heat.

Before serving add mint and cilantro leaf. Pour the entire dish into a large, deep serving bowl with ladle. Drizzle a small amount of Mango Sherry Sauce and Arugula oil over the top.

NOTE:
We serve this dish family style with warm crusty French baguette and Artisan butter.

WATERMELON SALAD

KAREN CARRIER

SERVES 4

- 1 SMALL SEEDLESS WATERMELON, RED OR YELLOW
- 1 POUND FRENCH FETA
- 1 BUNCH FRESH MINT, LEAVES ONLY
- 1 BUNCH FRESH THAI BASIL, LEAVES ONLY
- JUICE OF 2 LIMES
- ZEST OF 1 LIME
- 2 TEASPOONS SEA SALT
- 4 TABLESPOONS EXTRA VIRGIN OLIVE OIL

Cut watermelon into triangles leaving rind on. Arrange on a plate.

Drizzle lime juice over watermelon. Crumble feta cheese on top. Tear mint and Thai basil and sprinkle over salad.

Drizzle with olive oil. Sprinkle salt and lime zest over salad; serve.

Watermelon Salad, family style.

VINTAGE AMERICANA

MEMPHIS IS A CITY OF NEIGHBORHOODS. From South Main to Cooper-Young and Soulsville to High Point Terrace, Memphians take pride in their neighborhoods. Tucked away in Midtown is Edgewood Park Cove, a mini-neighborhood pulsating with six passionate hosts. Their coveted cove was the setting of a magical evening that featured four food trucks, a photo booth and local songstress Kait Lawson. The old-fashioned, yet chic nod to a backyard party of southern comfort inspired the name for this fete—Vintage Americana.

When Mary Allison and Andy Cates, Sally and Ashley Pace, Lynn and Jonathan Rowe, and Andrea and Allen Schwager were asked about the possibility of hosting a party to benefit the arts in their private cove, they embraced the idea wholeheartedly. All young families who are deeply involved and who love to celebrate Memphis, they welcomed the idea of converting their cove into a warm, inviting block party with local culinary delicacies served up truck to table. As Ashley explains, "Our neighborhood represents well the vibe of Midtown. We are an eclectic group of neighbors that has become a small group of friends who are willing to do anything for one another at a moment's notice. Having a cove setting gives us a spot to hang out, watch the kids play, or enjoy a late afternoon cocktail together near the fountain. Memphis is such a liveable city with so much to offer, and our neighborhood ties it all together for us."

"Memphis is such a liveable city with so much to offer, and our neighborhood ties it all together for us." –Ashley Pace

Stylists JJ Keras and Kerri Snead created a scene for the evening that was simultaneously retro and modern. As JJ explains, "The red door on one of the houses inspired the theme when we were trying to come up with a color scheme." Borrowing from the collection of Karlee Hickman, owner of Propcellar Vintage Rentals, the detail-intensive décor showcased strategically scouted pieces: garden stands, quilts and old phonographs.

Guests arrived to find a perfectly curated bar, including the evening's signature drink. "The specialty drink was bourbon, amaretto and soda," JJ describes. "It was delicious. Josh Hammond of Buster's Liquors & Wines came up with the recipe." The bar itself was a site to behold. Jamie Harmon, proprietor of the photo truck Amurica, lent his very red photo booth-toting, antique Volkswagen pick up. "Belly up to the truck" was the order of the night where the bartending couple extraordinaire Katie McWeeney and Abe Powell slung delicious drinks all night in their appropriately Americana denim shirts.

Food trucks served up all-American classics with a modern twist. The very hip, fresh pea green Graze Food Truck, a 1983 Chevy Step Van owned by Amelia Timms and Georgia Smith, was on site with a winter salad with warm apple cider vinaigrette, homemade chicken potpie, chili and beef stew. As Amelia explains of her inspiration for the menu, "We tried to go back to seasonal and local with the concept of the Vintage Americana theme. As a kid, I remember my mom making delicious potpies, old fashioned, very delicious American foods. The deconstructed potpie was a little more mobile and creative. I just wanted people to get it in their hands and feel cozy as they ate it. The butternut squash was perfectly in season at that time. I went back to my childhood and some of my comfort foods. I remember as a kid those foods made my heart warm when I ate them.

Autumn harvest on display.

Elizabeth Smithers, Margaret Frazier

Food Truck

⸗MENU⸗

—BURGUNDY BEEF STEW

—CHICKEN POT PIE W/PUFF
PASTRY

—ABOVE SERVED W/ WHIPPED
BABY RED POTATOES & FRESH
GREENS W/ROASTED BUTTERNUT
SQUASH & APPLE CIDER
VINAIGRETTE

—VEGETARIAN BLACK BEAN
CHILI

Abe Powell and Katie McWeeney serve up new and old favorites from the very unique, red pick-up truck 'bar'.

The Fuel Food Truck, a local favorite and an all natural restaurant and food truck, served a beet salad, naan prepared on-site and a lamb tagine stew, the perfect remedy for a chilly fall evening. Fuel Café and Food Truck owner Erik Proveaux describes the inspiration behind his truck. "I'd say it's all natural Americana," he says. "And that came from the fact that we're in an old 1920s gas station that we've refurbished. I've always been committed to all natural food with a modern twist." Rounding out the circle of food wagons, Revival Southern Food Company owned by Kathy McKee, prepared down-home favorites, including chicken pumpkin chowder, Mexican cornbread muffins, pot roast sliders, twice baked potatoes, BLT cheesecake bites and stuffed jalapeño poppers.

Muddy's Bake Shop, founded by native Memphian Kat Gordon, served dessert. The wildly popular, delightful and delicious business specializes in sweet goods, community service and a deep dedication to Memphis. Kat and her brother Kip made sure guests tried a little bit of all of their confections, including mini cherry pies, banana pudding, mini cupcakes, oatmeal cream pies and cranberry apple hand pies, made exclusively for the event. The Vintage Americana theme was a natural fit for Kat. "My favorite food is pie so we really wanted to bring the pies into it," she explains. "The night was a blast. The most difficult part was narrowing down the menu." The self-described "president of awesome" wore a homemade cherry pie hat perched perfectly askew and seriously awesome!

Guests meandered between the mobile food stations, sampling some of everything and queuing up for seconds and thirds of their favorites. As Amelia remembers, "It was cool to see people come back. One gentleman came back four or five times for the vegan chili, and that's just the best feeling ever."

The communal feel of the party was reflected in the chefs' thoughts about the food scene in Memphis. "There is so much excitement in Memphis right now with food," Kat explains. "Memphis is a big small town. We all know each other. I love that while the food industry has grown, it has kept that same sense of community. Every person in every aspect of food service in Memphis is a team player. You have this wonderful sense of camaraderie. I think it's something really, really special compared to other cities."

Local singer songwriter Kait Lawson provided the entertainment for the evening. A Memphis native, Kait has lived and worked in Nashville and New York, but returned to Memphis to record her debut album *Until We Drown*. Her sound is soulful and smooth, and rooted in Southern influences. The deep and personal lyrics of *Memphis*-"Seen the Grand Canyon, seen the Great Lakes, I've been to New York and I almost stayed, but I know where I belong; Memphis you're my home"—capture the exciting sense of energy around the city's authentic music scene and surely captured the hearts of this midtown Memphis neighborhood.

Throughout the evening, guests preened and posed in Jamie Harmon's Amurica photo booth. It is only fitting that Harmon, born on a levee near Greenville, Mississippi in the back of a 1966 four-door silver Chevy Corvair, began his photo business in a mobile camper, a silver one, in fact. A fixture at weddings, birthday parties and festivals, the trailer-style photo booth is just wacky enough, with a wardrobe and props department that would be the envy of any wardrobe technician. Pose, click and *presto*: prints within seconds, a perfect party favor and Americana captured.

The party did unfortunately have to come to an end, but its hosts remember it fondly. As Andy Cates recounts, "It was amazing how fast the party came together in an afternoon and came down an hour after the event. Clearly there was a ton of energy and time spent prior to the event to make it a success." Sally Pace sums it up best from beginning to end. "What a magical event," she says. "We were able to provide a backdrop for an evening with an Americana vibe, and no detail was left out. From the local food trucks that served guests to the big screen featuring Indie Memphis films, and from the sounds of Kait Lawson on stage to the photo-ops at the Amurica photo booth, it was a casual night that showcased some of the very best talent Memphis has to offer. This setting allowed the crowd to really get a taste for the variety of ways that ArtsMemphis enhances the community."

"There is so much excitement in Memphis right now with food. Memphis is a big small town. We all know each other." –Kat Gordon

Stylist, Kerri Snead

Fuel Café chef John Sawrie

L to r: Kathy McKee and Holly Taylor

Graze Food Truck's very hip, pea green truck.

Hay bales with vintage quilts provide seating around the cove's fountain.

Stylist, JJ Keras, "We're always building up the Memphis community when we work together on events like this."

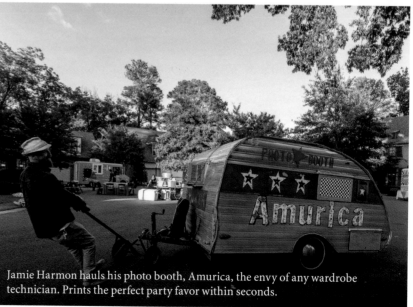

Jamie Harmon hauls his photo booth, Amurica, the envy of any wardrobe technician. Prints the perfect party favor within seconds.

Did this squirrel crash the party?!!!!

Al Gamble and Kait Lawson

Holly Taylor and Cathy McKee choose just the right accessory for their close-up.

Kip and Kat Gordon

Kat Gordon sporting her cherry pie chapeau.

Abe Powell, Katie McWeeney

Naan prepared on site by David Frink.

Flattened and shaped naan bread baking in cylindrical oven.

David Frink.

Stuffed jalapeño peppers by Revival Southern Food Truck.

Pot roast sliders by Revival Southern Food Truck.

A harvest moon shone on the party scene.

Kait Lawson, along with Al Gamble, performed her smooth and soulful sounds for the guests.

The red door inspired the color theme.

L to r: Kelly Bridgforth, Barry Bridgforth

Dynisha Woods, Kevin Woods, Ashley and husband Todd Tobias

Megan and Steele Ford

The bonfire, a gathering place for warmth and good spirit.

Wren Cates, Mary Allison Cates

William Pace and Ashley Pace –
A good time was had by guests of all ages.

Queuing up for the irresistibly tasty truck food.

L to r: Gary Backaus, Margot McNeeley, Jeff Edwards, Sally Pace

L to r: Kevin Woods, Mary Trotz, Joanna Lipman, Scott Baum

Kait Lawson

DECONSTRUCTED CHICKEN POT PIE

AMELIA TIMMS

- 5 CUPS CHICKEN STOCK
- 2 CHICKEN BOUILLON CUBES
- 1½ STICKS UNSALTED BUTTER
- 2 CUPS CHOPPED YELLOW ONIONS (2 ONIONS)
- ¾ CUP ALL-PURPOSE FLOUR
- 2 TEASPOONS SALT
- ½ TEASPOON PEPPER
- ½ CUP HEAVY CREAM
- 6 BONELESS, SKINLESS, POACHED, CHICKEN BREAST, SHREDDED
- 2 CUPS MEDIUM-DICED CARROTS, BLANCHED FOR 2 MINUTES
- 1 (10 OUNCE) PACKAGE FROZEN PEAS (2 CUPS)
- ½ CUP CHOPPED FRESH PARSLEY
- 1 TABLESPOON CHOPPED FRESH THYME LEAVES
- 1 PACKAGE PREPARED PUFF PASTRY SHEETS
- FLOUR FOR DUSTING FLAT SURFACE

Preheat oven to 375 degrees.

In a small saucepan, heat chicken stock and dissolve bouillon cubes in the stock.

In a large pot, melt butter and sauté onions over medium-low heat for 10-15 minutes, until translucent. Add flour and cook over low heat, stirring constantly, for 2 minutes.

Add chicken stock to the pot. Simmer over low heat for 1 more minute, stirring until thick. Add salt, pepper and heavy cream; stir to combine. Add chicken, carrots, peas, parsley and thyme. Mix well.

Open puff pastry sheets and lay out on floured flat surface. Use open end of round drinking glass, or round metal cookie cutter to cut out shapes for your potpie top. Have fun with the shapes. I sometimes use stars or flower cutters.

Spoon filling equally in ovenproof bowls. Top each bowl with cut out puff pastry topper. Place bowls on baking sheet and bake until the top is golden brown and the filling is bubbling hot. Enjoy!!

LAMB TAGINE

ERIK PROVEAUX

- 2 POUNDS BONELESS LEG OF LAMB, CUT INTO 1 INCH CUBES
- 4 TABLESPOONS RES-EN-HANOUT (ALSO CALLED 7 SPICE, IT'S A MOROCCAN SPICE BLEND)
- ¼ CUP FLOUR WITH SALT AND PEPPER FOR DUSTING LAMB
- OLIVE OIL
- 1½ CUPS DICED YELLOW ONIONS
- 6 CLOVES GARLIC CHOPPED
- 1 CUP WHITE WINE
- 2 MEDIUM CARROTS CUT INTO ½ INCH CHUNKS
- ½ CUP DRIED APRICOTS CUT INTO ¼ INCH SLICES
- ½ CUP GOLDEN RAISINS
- 2 TABLESPOONS HONEY
- 1 CAN CHICKPEAS
- 1 CINNAMON STICK
- 1 TABLESPOON CHOPPED FRESH GINGER
- 1 CAN DICED TOMATOES
- 2 CUPS CHICKEN OR VEGETABLE STOCK

SERVE WITH:

- COUSCOUS
- BASMATI RICE
- TOASTED PITA
- NAAN BREAD

GARNISH:

- FRESH CILANTRO
- POMEGRANATE SEEDS
- TOASTED SLICED ALMONDS

Season lamb cubes with spice mixture and refrigerate overnight.

Dust lamb with seasoned flour. Preheat a heavy gauge Dutch oven, preferably enamel coated or stainless steel, on medium heat for about 1 minute, then add olive oil to coat the bottom of the pan. Raise heat to high. The oil will ripple and just start to smoke. Add lamb without crowding and brown on at least two sides. Remove browned lamb to a plate. Pour off oil and add a few more tablespoons of fresh oil; return the pan to medium-high heat. Add onions and garlic. Sauté for a few minutes without browning the garlic too much. Deglaze with white wine; let it boil and reduce some. Return lamb to pot and add remaining ingredients; cover and simmer on low for around 2½ hours.

Check mixture along the way to make sure it doesn't burn on the bottom. You might need to add more water. It works well to bake in a oven instead of simmering. This recipe works in a crock-pot, as well.

After 2½ hours, check to see if the lamb is tender. It should be tender but not falling apart. Adjust salt and pepper.

Serve over couscous, basmati rice, or with toasted pita or Naan bread. Garnish with cilantro, pomegranate seeds, or toasted almonds.

GRAZE CHIPS

AMELIA TIMMS

- 4 CUPS (2 SERVINGS) THIN SLICED PAN-FRIED CRISPY POTATO CHIPS
- ½ CUP GREEK SALAD DRESSING
- ¼ CUP CRUMBLED FETA CHEESE
- ¼ CUP DICED RED ONION
- ¼ CUP SLICED BLACK OLIVES
- ½ CUP SLICED CHERRY TOMATOES
- ½ CUP DICED ENGLISH CUCUMBER

Plate chips curled side up and drizzle chips with Greek dressing. Top chips with remaining ingredients, Enjoy!!

NOTE:
These are one of our most popular dishes on the Graze truck; so simple, but so delicious!

STRAWBERRY RHUBARB PIE WITH CRUMBLE TOPPING

KAT GORDON

THIS WILL WIN FRIENDS AND INFLUENCE PEOPLE!

THE PIE...

- 1 UNBAKED PIE CRUST, 9 OR 10 INCHES
- 3 CUPS SLICED STRAWBERRIES
- 2 CUPS CHOPPED FRESH RHUBARB
- ½ CUP SUGAR
- ½ CUP LIGHT BROWN SUGAR
- ¼ CUP FLOUR
- 2 TABLESPOONS CORNSTARCH
- 1 TEASPOON CINNAMON
- 1 TEASPOON VANILLA
- 1 TEASPOON LEMON JUICE

THE CRUMBLE TOPPING...

- ⅓ CUP LIGHT BROWN SUGAR
- ¼ CUP FLOUR
- ½ CUP OATS
- ¼ CUP SOFTENED BUTTER
- ¼ CUP CHOPPED PECANS
- ¼ CUP SLICED ALMONDS
- ½ TEASPOON CINNAMON
- DASH OF FINE SEA SALT

Preheat oven to 400 degrees.

Roll out 1 pie crust and fit to pie pan. (If you want to cheat and use a pre-made one, I won't tell anyone — just make sure it's excellent "quality!") Chill.

Dump strawberries and rhubarb into large bowl and gently toss with sugars, flour, cornstarch, cinnamon, vanilla, and lemon juice. Allow to sit for 15-30 minutes.

Using a slotted spoon, transfer the fruit filling into the chilled pie shell. Discard the leftover 'juice'. Return pie to ice box while making crumble topping.

Thoroughly combine all the ingredients for the crumble, then evenly distribute across the top of the pie.

Freeze the pie for 20 minutes (see Note below).

Place pie on parchment-lined baking sheet. Bake 20 minutes and then reduce heat to 350 degrees and bake for another 40 minutes or until crust is golden and juices are bubbling.

Cool thoroughly before serving, at least 2 hours.

NOTE:
At this point, you may actually choose to freeze the pie and bake it later. After its initial 20 minute "cool off", remove it from the freezer and wrap it tightly in several layers of plastic wrap, and then place it inside a large freezer ziptop. It will keep for about 2 months in the freezer. When you're ready to bake it, just put it directly in the oven and bake as instructed — it may take slightly longer. This is perfect if you're serving it to a crowd and want to do the bulk of the preparation ahead of time!

APPLE CRANBERRY PARTY PIE

KAT GORDON

- ½ CUP SUGAR
- ¼ TEASPOON CINNAMON
- ¼ TEASPOON FINE SEA SALT
- 1 TABLESPOON CORNSTARCH
- 6 APPLES, PEELED, CORED, AND SLICED — USE A MIX OF VARIETIES, SOME TART, SOME SWEET
- YOUR FAVORITE PIE DOUGH RECIPE, ENOUGH FOR A TYPICAL DOUBLE CRUST PIE
- 1½ CUPS CRANBERRY SAUCE (WE MAKE OURS, BUT YOU CAN USE CANNED TO SAVE TIME OR YOUR FAVORITE HOMEMADE RECIPE!)
- 1 EGG YOLK FOR EGG WASH
- 2 TABLESPOONS MILK OR CREAM
- SUGAR FOR SPRINKLING ON TOPS

Preheat the oven to 400 degrees.

In a large, microwave-safe bowl, combine sugar, cinnamon, salt, and cornstarch. Add apple slices and toss well.

Microwave on high for 3 minutes, then stir. Repeat 2 more times or until apples are softened but not mushy. Cool to room temperature.

Once cool, process slightly in a food processor so chunks of apple are about the size of butter beans or nickels.

While the apple mixture cools, roll out the pie dough to between ⅛ and ¼ inch thick.

Use a biscuit cutter or large-ish round cookie cutter to cut as many rounds as possible in the dough. Place half of these on parchment covered cookie sheets.

TO ASSEMBLE HAND PIES...

Spoon a teaspoon of cranberry sauce onto each dough round, then spoon about 1 tablespoon of apple filling on top of that.

Brush a bit of ice water on the edges of the pie dough, then place the other round on top and gently press the edges together. Crimp with a fork to seal.

Brush all the little hand pies with egg wash (1 egg yolk plus 2 tablespoons milk or cream, whisked together) and sprinkle with sugar. Cut small vents so steam can escape.

Put the pies in the freezer for about 30 minutes. (You can keep these frozen for up to 2 months if you'd like to prepare ahead of time and serve later!)

To bake, make sure the hand pies are spaced about 1-2 inches apart from each other on parchment covered cookie sheets.

Bake at 400 degrees for about 13 minutes, then rotate sheets and reduce heat to 350 degrees.

Bake another 20 minutes or until juices are bubbling.

Allow to cool, then serve! Yum!

WATCH YO HED

MEMPHIS IS A GRITTY CITY WITH A HISTORY THAT RUNS DEEP. It is comfortable with the high and the low, reveling in the contradictions and juxtapositions between the two. So when chefs Kelly English of Restaurant Iris and The Second Line, Patrick Reilly of the Majestic Grille and Jason Severs of Bari Ristorante e Enoteca decided to prepare an upscale, authentically Memphis dinner together, there was no spot more iconic or fitting than Earnestine & Hazel's. Exposed brick walls, broken tile floors and cracked sheet rock characterize the notorious dive bar known for having the most soulful jukebox and burgers in the world. This perfectly imperfect scene was the ideal setting for an elegant, yet appropriately raucous dinner party named for the tellingly rough-hewn sign that adorns a too-low passageway, reminding the amateur or simply careless guest to "Watch Yo Hed."

The legendary bar commonly referred to as "Earnestine's" began as a pharmacy in the 1930s, and since it has been a de facto hair salon, sundry store, café, music club, brothel and restaurant. It is believed to be haunted by Earnestine and Hazel, the ghosts of long dead hairstylists for whom it is named. After considering several other iconic Memphis spots, the chefs settled on Earnestine's because, as Kelly recounts, "We talked about juxtaposition. We were going to be in this place that's so urban and imperfect, so for us to put out these perfect little courses that are so technical would be neat. That juxtaposition, to me, is Memphis."

Earnestine's sits in the heart of Memphis' South Main Arts District. Home to historic Memphis spots like the National Civil Rights Museum at the Lorraine Motel, the Arcade Restaurant and former Central Train Station, South Main is a uniquely Memphis neighborhood. Imperfect sidewalks run along historic buildings that have been kept architecturally intact since the turn of the 20th century. While the district fell into disrepair in the wake of Dr. Martin Luther King, Jr's assassination, in the past decade it has enjoyed a renaissance with residential, commercial and artistic development, and is now a gem of Memphis' up-and-coming cultural landscape and comeback story.

> "We were going to be in this place that's so urban and imperfect, so for us to put out these perfect little courses that are so technical would be neat. That juxtaposition to me is Memphis."
> –Kelly English

Guests for the evening entered through the South Main Street door and, even though it was a Monday night, they immediately felt the energy in the room. The front bar hummed with excitement as eager customers saddled up to the legendary bar for the first drink of the night. Patrick notes that like other nights, "When there's a crowd at Earnestine's, it's magic when you walk in. It has an energy that nowhere else has. You walk in and you think, 'I'm here to party'."

Bari Ristorante bartender Brad Pitts served up a host of delicious libations for the evening, starting with generous pours of champagne paired with Kelly's raw oyster appetizer. As Kelly recounts, "When we were planning the menu, we talked about high and low, and so I was thinking about fancy

KELLY ENGLISH

KELLY ENGLISH is the Executive Chef and owner of Restaurant Iris and The Second Line in Memphis. His culinary style incorporates familiar flavors from his childhood in southern Louisiana into French-Creole cuisine. A graduate of the Culinary Institute of America, he spent several years training under John Besh in New Orleans before moving to Memphis to open Restaurant Iris. In 2009 Kelly celebrated the restaurant's first anniversary by being named one of Food & Wine's "Best New Chefs." He was also a 2010 James Beard Award nominee for "Best Chef: Southeast." Kelly was a featured chef in *Wild Abundance: Ritual, Revelry and Recipes from the South's Finest Hunting Clubs.*

PATRICK REILLY

PATRICK REILLY is the Executive Chef and owner of The Majestic Grille in Memphis. A native of Dublin, Ireland, Patrick studied at the Dublin College of Catering and Hotel Management before apprenticing at the Brewers' Dining Hall at the Guinness Storehouse Dublin. He worked in restaurants in London, New York, Chicago and Orlando before opening The Lounge at Gibson Guitar Factory. He is the President of the Memphis Restaurant Association.

JASON SEVERS

JASON SEVERS is the Executive Chef and owner of Bari Ristorante e Enoteca and Three Angels Diner in Memphis. A Tennessee native, Severs' food is inspired by his Italian and Mediterranean roots. His style of cuisine focuses on fresh ingredients and simple, refined preparation.

L to r: Chefs Kelly English, Jason Severs, Patrick Reilly

"When there's a crowd at Earnestine's, it's magic when you walk in. It has an energy that nowhere else has. You walk in and you're like, 'I'm here to party.'" –Patrick Reilly

ingredients. To me there's nothing fancier than eating raw oysters and caviar: eggs and oysters. We made a little mignonette with some vodka. I wanted people to have to slurp it out of the shell and not use a cocktail fork because that brought it back to the level of what Earnestine & Hazel's is."

As attendees sipped and slurped, they were treated to an original performance by Project: Motion Modern Dance Collective. A local company, Project: Motion is known for their experimental, movement-based art. For Watch Yo Hed, they created a sexy, sultry piece inspired by Earnestine & Hazel's storied history and its appropriately greasy Soul Burger. A soulful dance performance called for appropriately soulful music, and local legend Blind Mississippi Morris gave guests a taste of real Memphis blues, even if he was wearing a bright green suit.

The Soul Burger also inspired the chefs. Originally, they planned to prepare their own takes on the dish, but decided that they really could not improve on such a good thing. Instead, they embraced high cuisine, preparing duck foie gras pate with brichoe, lamb and fish. As Jason explains, "We all kept saying the word juxtaposition.

"The walls were talking, it was a beaten and polished reflection of the area. It looked very Delta." –Jason Severs

We were all on the same wavelength without planning it. We wanted it to be high-end food at a dive."

The chefs' vision was also central to transforming the Five Spot, a normally low-key dining area behind the main bar, into a dramatic, beautiful space. Jason recalls, "The look of the party was a reflection of the area. It looked and felt very Delta." Stylists Grant Ray, Hayley Davis and Kerri Snead ensured that the décor was on point and the details attended to, from the whimsical menu design to centerpieces that included succulents in spray painted metal cans to the much-loved "Watch Yo Hed" kitchen towels that guests received as party favors. In keeping with the theme for the evening, the dining room was not a perfect, restaurant-worthy space. Instead, the floor was uneven, the warm temperature encouraged guests to take off their dinner jackets, and a banana spider adorned the wall.

After dinner the chefs gave a toast, were toasted by attendees and answered questions from the crowd. Their spirit of collaboration was evident, as Patrick remembers, "When you get in your own kitchen, you don't learn a lot. When you do these events, you get

to learn from other chefs." Kelly also emphasized the cooperative spirit of Memphis' culinary scene, "We're at a time now when everyone is really comfortable sharing what they do. Now chefs' personalities are in their restaurants. I don't feel uncomfortable sharing anything we do at Iris."

Like any good night at Earnestine's, the party moved upstairs for drinks and dessert. The movement of the party was by design, as Kelly explains, "We would usually start downstairs, move upstairs, hang out in that front room and on the way out, we'd have a burger and it was time to go." Profiteroles, butternut squash squares and other treats were served on silver platters in the various extra rooms of the upstairs.

Delta blues chanteuse Eden Brent played the funky, old piano and sang favorite tunes to go with guests' after dinner libations. Brad prepared a special, slushy punch for the night, referred to as "Stand Up Punch," because if you drink it sitting down, you will not be able to stand up. As he explains, serving drinks at Earnestine's was an honor. "It's not just the drink mixing part, it's the experience of hanging out at the restaurant and having a drink. To be asked to stand behind the bar at Earnestine's was an honor. I don't know many people who can say that they've done that." He shared the upstairs bar with Nate, longtime bartender in residence at the eponymous Nate's Bar, known for strong drinks and a come-one, come-all attitude.

Despite the fact that it was a Monday night, guests kept raging until past the midnight hour. Soul Burgers served on silver trays provided much needed sustenance and helped everyone to stand up, even despite the punch. Everyone left in high spirits, knowing that the night was a true once-in-a-lifetime experience.

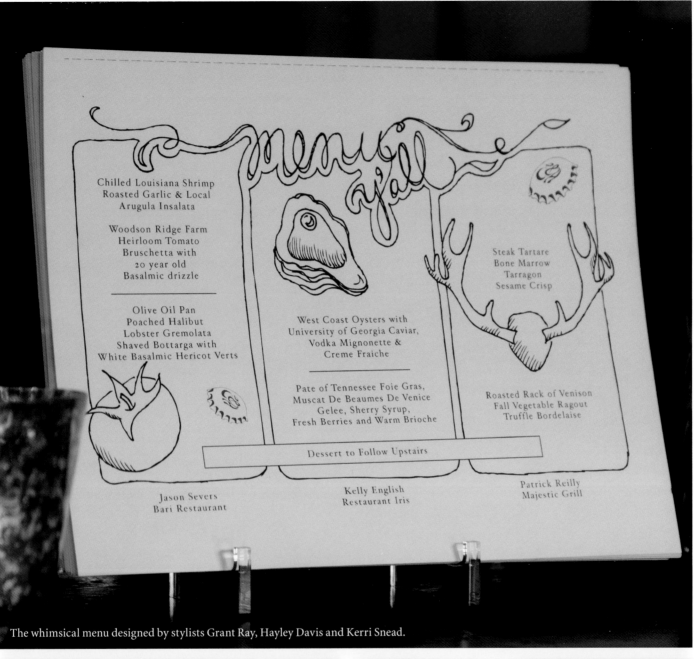

menu y'all

Chilled Louisiana Shrimp
Roasted Garlic & Local
Arugula Insalata

Woodson Ridge Farm
Heirloom Tomato
Bruschetta with
20 year old
Basalmic drizzle

Olive Oil Pan
Poached Halibut
Lobster Gremolata
Shaved Bottarga with
White Basalmic Hericot Verts

West Coast Oysters with
University of Georgia Caviar,
Vodka Mignonette &
Creme Fraiche

Pate of Tennessee Foie Gras,
Muscat De Beaumes De Venice
Gelee, Sherry Syrup,
Fresh Berries and Warm Brioche

Steak Tartare
Bone Marrow
Tarragon
Sesame Crisp

Roasted Rack of Venison
Fall Vegetable Ragout
Truffle Bordelaise

Dessert to Follow Upstairs

Jason Severs
Bari Restaurant

Kelly English
Restaurant Iris

Patrick Reilly
Majestic Grill

The whimsical menu designed by stylists Grant Ray, Hayley Davis and Kerri Snead.

"Kitchy" towel party favors.

A sight for soulful eyes.

Stylist, Kerri Snead

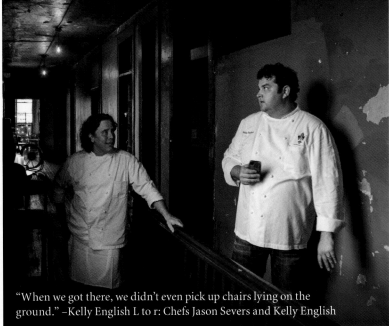

"When we got there, we didn't even pick up chairs lying on the ground." –Kelly English L to r: Chefs Jason Severs and Kelly English

Stylists, Hayley Davis and Grant Ray

"We tried to ensure that the unique ambiance of Earnestine and Hazels was left intact, and we played off that." –Stylist, Grant Ray

There's nothing fancier than eating raw oysters and caviar: eggs and oysters. We made a little mignonette with some vodka. I wanted people to have to slurp it out of the shell and not use a cocktail fork because that brought it back to the level of what Earnestine & Hazel's is."
–Kelly English
Photo: Lindsey Hammond

Angela English

Chef Kelly English

Sally Pace and her husband, Ashley

L to r: Margaret Shivers, Grant Ray, Michael Shivers, Mark Jordan

Delta Blues great, Blind Mississippi Morris, rated one of the best 10 harmonica players in the world.

Project: Motion Dance Collective created a sexy, sultry piece inspired by Earnestine & Hazel's storied history and its appropriately greasy Soul Burger.

Blind Mississippi Morris and Frank Monteleone

Joan Biddle and husband, Jacob, Greg Baudoin

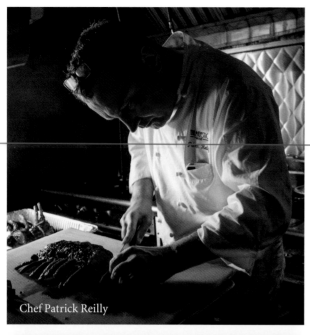

Chef Patrick Reilly

Chef Kelly English

"We look out for each other." L to r: Chefs, Patrick Reilly, Kelly English, Jason Severs

The tellingly rough-hewn sign that adorns a too-low passageway, reminding the amateur or simply careless guest to "Watch Yo Hed."

The old Christmas lights were left in place and the crystal chandeliers were hung to achieve that juxtaposition that the chefs were looking for.

Grit and Grace.

The Chefs deliver more than a feast, good-hearted humor is also on their menu. L to r: Susan Schadt, Chefs Kelly English, Patrick Reilly and Jason Severs

L to r: Matt Parker, John Robinson, Sam Nevels, McCown Smith

Josh Hammond paying tribute to the former owner of E & H, Russell George

L to r: McCown Smith, Sam Nevels, Bob Craddock and his wife Deborah.

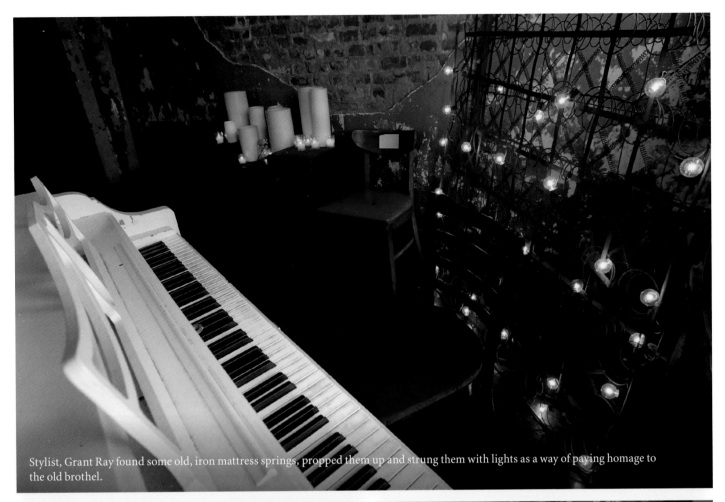

Stylist, Grant Ray found some old, iron mattress springs, propped them up and strung them with lights as a way of paying homage to the old brothel.

A peek into Nate's Bar. L to r: Nate and Annie Bares

Delta blues chanteuse Eden Brent and Chef Patrick Reilly.

Nate, a one-name celebrity.

Guests partake of Brad Pitts' *Stand Up Punch*. Brad, the popular bartender at Bari was asked to stand behind the bar at Earnestine's and shared the upstairs bar with Nate. "It was an honor. I don't know many people who can say that they've done that."

The soul burger brigade. L to r: Brad Pitts, Rebecca Severs, Chef Patrick Reilly, Clarence Connelly, Chef Jason Severs, Chef Kelly English, Angela English, Deni Reilly

L to r: Eden Brent, Deborah and Bob Craddock, Lindsey and Josh Hammond

The mighty Soul Burger.

Culinary school at E&H. L to r: Chefs Jason Severs, Patrick Reilly, Keenan Harding

Did somebody say "juxtaposition?" Justin DeGroff

Rebecca and husband, Chef Jason Severs.

GULF OYSTERS WITH CATHEAD MIGNONETTE AND CAVIAR

KELLY ENGLISH

Serves 4

- ½ cup cathead vodka
- ½ cup red wine vinegar
- ½ cup finely diced shallots
- 1 tablespoon freshly ground black pepper
- 48 gulf oysters
- ½ cup crème fraîche
- 1 ounce caviar, as fancy as you want it to be

To make the mignonette, place vodka, vinegar, shallots and pepper in a saucepan. Bring to a boil. Cut off heat and chill.

Carefully wash oysters and then crack them. Be careful not to damage oyster but be sure to separate them from both sides of the shell, leaving oyster in the half of the shell that will serve best as a cup. Arrange on trays of ice.

Top each oyster with a spoonful of mignonette, a dab of crème fraîche, and a small amount of caviar. Eat and enjoy life.

CHILLED SHRIMP BRUSCHETTA WITH LOCAL HEIRLOOM TOMATOES INSALATA AND LOCAL ARUGULA PESTO

JASON SEVERS

- ¼ POUND SMALL TO MEDIUM SHRIMP PEELED AND DEVEINED
- 3-4 LOCAL HEIRLOOM TOMATOES (USE 3 TO 4 DIFFERENT VARIETIES)
- EXTRA VIRGIN OLIVE OIL
- KOSHER SALT AND FRESHLY GROUND BLACK PEPPER
- FRESH BASIL
- ½ POUND OF LOCAL ARUGULA
- 1 ANCHOVY FILLET
- 1 CLOVE GARLIC, MINCED
- 1 LOAF OF NICE, CRUSTY BREAD OF YOUR CHOICE
- AGED BALSAMIC VINEGAR

Add shrimp to a pot of boiling water and cook for approximately 3-4 minutes, or to your desired degree of doneness. Shock shrimp after cooking by draining and placing them in an ice bath. When cool, drain and chill.

Blanch tomatoes in boiling water for about 15 seconds; drain and immediately put in an ice bath. After cooled, drain and peel the skin off of tomatoes. After blanching them the skin should literally peel away with your fingers. After peeling, cut tomatoes in half and squeeze them gently over a receptacle, allowing the seeds and membrane inside to fall away.

Using a cutting board, dice tomatoes into small ¼ inch pieces. Place in a small bowl, drizzle with olive oil, and sprinkle a little kosher salt, black pepper. Tear or julienne the fresh basil and add to taste. Set aside.

In the bowl of a food processor, place arugula, anchovy, and garlic; blend together until resembles a very dry paste. With the processor running, slowly add olive oil until it comes together in a light emulsion. Add salt and pepper to taste. Set aside.

Slice bread into ½ inch slices and cut into small rounds, squares or triangles. Place bread under the broiler until it is nicely toasted.

Place chilled shrimp on their sides and make a complete cut length-wise, making two complete pieces of each shrimp.

Spread a small amount of pesto on each toast slice.

Place one piece of your chilled shrimp, cut side down, on each piece of toast.

Place a small amount of tomato salad on top of each shrimp.

Drizzle extra virgin olive oil and aged balsamic vinegar on top of each piece and serve immediately.

OLIVE OIL POACHED HALIBUT WITH LOBSTER GREMOLATA AND WHITE BALSAMIC GREEN BEANS

JASON SEVERS

SERVES 6

- 6 (5 OUNCE) PIECES OF FRESH HALIBUT, SKIN REMOVED
- EXTRA VIRGIN OLIVE OIL
- 1 POUND FRESH LOBSTER CLAW, KNUCKLE AND TAIL MEAT
- 6 LEMONS
- 1 BUNCH ITALIAN PARSLEY, LEAVES COARSELY CHOPPED
- 2 RIBS CELERY, CUT LENGTH-WISE AND THINLY SLICED
- 1 CLOVE GARLIC, CHOPPED
- 1 POUND BABY GREEN BEANS OR HARICOT VERTS
- WHITE BALSAMIC VINEGAR
- KOSHER SALT AND FRESHLY GROUND BLACK PEPPER

Preheat oven to 200 degrees. Place halibut in a shallow roasting pan and pour olive oil over it to almost cover the fish. Cover pan with foil tightly, and place in preheated oven for approximately 1 hour. Time will vary based on your personal preference, but after 1 hour, the fish should be completely cooked through.

While halibut is baking, sauté lobster meat for approximately 10 minutes in a small amount of olive oil over medium heat. Set aside to cool.

Juice 2 of the lemons and pour juice into a large bowl. Remove the rind, pith, seeds and membrane from the remaining 4 lemons. Cut the fruit in small pieces and add to the bowl of lemon juice. Add parsley, celery and garlic. Roughly chop cooled lobster meat until all of the pieces are about the size of a nickel. Add to the bowl of lemon mixture and drizzle with about 2 tablespoons of olive oil. Using a strong metal or wooden mixing spoon, combine well. Intermittently, use the side of spoon to "chop" the mixture in order to break up the lobster and lemons. Taste the mixture for balance, if too lemony, add some more oil, or vice versa. Add salt and pepper to taste, set aside for the flavors to blend.

Blanch green beans in boiling salted water for 1-2 minutes or until they are cooked al dente. Drain and place them in an ice bath immediately to cool. Drain and set aside.

When fish is cooked, heat a sauté pan to medium-high. Drizzle the pan with olive oil and add green beans. They should sizzle. Stir them to heat through and add about 3 tablespoons of white balsamic vinegar, and salt and pepper to taste. Toss together.

To serve, place around 7-8 green beans in the center of a dining plate and drizzle a little of the pan juices. Carefully remove the foil from the roasting pan of halibut and place one piece of halibut on top of the green beans. Top the halibut with a large spoonful of the lobster gremolata and drizzle the plate with olive oil.

STAND UP PUNCH

BRAD PITTS

It's called Stand Up Punch because you can't sit down and drink it!
Serves approximately 20 people

- 6-8 cups water
- 2 cups strongly brewed tea
- 2-3 cups bourbon (preferably sweeter bourbon/does not have to be expensive)
- 1 cup sugar
- 1 (6 ounce) container frozen orange juice concentrate, thawed
- 1 (6 ounce) container frozen lemonade concentrate, thawed
- 2 liters ginger ale
- garnish: mint sprig or lemon slices (optional)

Combine water, tea, bourbon, sugar, orange juice and lemonade concentrate, and ginger ale in large pot on low heat; mix until sugar dissolves. Let mixture cool until able to handle safely.

Carefully ladle or pour warm punch into gallon-sized freezer bags. Freeze for at least 36-48 hours. (This is important in order preserve it's consistency when served.)

When time to serve, place the frozen punch from the individual bags together in a large punch bowl and let thaw, breaking up every 15 minutes.

As punch melts, add some ginger ale if desired and garnish with fresh mint sprigs lemon slices.

STRONG TEA

Note:
This recipe can be doubled easily to serve at larger parties or modified as you see fit. I quadrupled it in order to serve at the ArtsMemphis benefit where it was thoroughly enjoyed by everyone, including me!

- 2 cups water
- 1 family-size or 4 regular tea bags

Boil the water and add tea bags and let steep until cool. Discard the tea bags before adding to punch mixture.

ACKNOWLEDGEMENTS

MEMPHIS
SWEET, SPICY & A LITTLE GREASY

Thirty-four chefs, eight hundred guests, twelve arts groups,
sixty performers, ten venues, twelve events—MAGICAL

ARTSMEMPHIS:

Lauren Boyer our creative magician with an amazing sense of style, she helps define, distinguish and elevate the ArtsMemphis brand. Throughout collateral materials, web site design and social media, her first priority was artistic purity for the artists and chefs, ensuring that *everything feels right*.

Parke Kennedy works logistical magic. Mastering the art of blending vision with business and facilitating the process to reality, Parke produced a variety of events ranging from intimate gatherings from 25 guests to large-scale productions for 150 people. A connector and negotiator, Parke embraces the mantra that *everything matters*.

Elizabeth Rouse possesses a secret magic that others want to share. She inspired the team with her leadership, exuberance, charisma and positive energy. With Elizabeth, *everything is authentic*.

WIMMER COOKBOOKS:

Doug McNeill, Vice President of Wimmer Cookbooks, serves up magic daily with his team; Jennifer Allison, Maureen Fortune and Melanie Thompson. Add to the mix a heaping portion of donated time, requisite patience and professional guidance and we got *everything cooked to perfection*.

RECIPE AND TEXT EDITOR:

Kay Carey, who magically oozes the joy of cooking, a trait neither Annie Bares, my co-writer, nor I possess. She recently produced a beautiful cookbook, *Hearts of Palm: Boca Grand Cooks,* with Wimmer Cookbooks and can identify a flaw in a recipe as quickly as my soufflés would surely fall (if I should attempt one). Kay filled in the gaps from food expertise to literary editing and *everything in between*.

FAMILY AND FRIENDS:

Once again my family and friends realized that this book had, in the words of a dear friend, "Stolen my heart". That means saying "no" sometimes. Events, deadlines, chefs, sponsors, and donors all deserve the best product ArtsMemphis can deliver. So to our daughters, friends and especially to my husband Chuck, thank you for your patience, *you guys are my everything*.

SUSAN SCHADT

2013 ARTSMEMPHIS
CULINARY SERIES SPONSORS

BEAUTY AND THE FEAST: LOVE ON THE INSTALLMENT PLAN

CULINARY DINNER SERIES 2013

PRESENTED BY WUNDERLICH SECURITIES

BOOK SPONSOR: WIMMER COOKBOOKS

Athens Distributing Company

Baker, Donelson, Bearman, Caldwell & Berkowitz PC

Buster's Wines & Liquors

BuzzFREE Mosquito Control

Christopher Cooley DDS

Cornerstone Cellars | Stepping Stone Cellars

Cushman & Wakefield | Commercial Advisors

Farm Truck Organics & Groceries

Fish and Associates

Garden District

High Tech Special Effects

Holliday Flowers & Events

Howell Marketing Strategies LLC

Hyde Family Foundations

inbalance fitness

Kiser's Floor Fashions

LifeLinc Anesthesia

Mahaffey Tent & Party Rentals

Mona Spa & Wellness

Paulsen Printing Company

Propcellar Vintage Rentals

Red Door Wealth Management

Ruch Clinic

Shindigs by Sheril

Whole Foods Market

RESOURCE GUIDE

BE NICE OR LEAVE
Alexa Pulitzer: Placecards | alexapulitzer.com
Brave Designs: Boutonnieres and headdresses
Buster's Liquors & Wines: Alcoholic beverages | bustersliquors.com
Café Las Flores: Coffee | cafelasflores.com
Garden District: Flower arrangements, tree centerpieces, hanging lanterns | gardendistrictmemphis.com
Jeremy Shrader Quartet & Mighty Souls Brass Band: Music | jeremyshradermusic.com
Lake's Catfish: Catfish filets | 662.363.1847
Mahaffey Tent & Event Rentals: Tent, tables, chairs, chair pads, silverware, glasses | mahaffeytent.com
Opera Memphis: Music | operamemphis.org
Sheri McKelvie: English muffins | cucinabread.com
Uglesich's Restaurant Cookbook & Gail's Rémoulade Sauce | www.uglesichs.com
Whole Foods Market: Food purveyor | wholefoodsmarket.com

FOXFIELD
Buster's Liquors & Wines: Alcoholic beverages | bustersliquors.com
Claybrook Farms: Baron of beef | claybrookangus.com
Dennis Paullus: Wood turning | dennispaullus.pro
Farm Truck Organics: Food purveyor | farmtruckorganics.com
Garden District: Arbor, chandeliers, chairs (Saturday night), linens (Saturday night), lanterns, floral arrangements, event styling | gardendistrictmemphis.com
High Tech Special Effects: Fireworks | hightechspecialeffects.com
Kent Walker Cheese: Cheese | kentwalkercheese.com
Lisa Hudson: Pottery | 901.378.9767
Mahaffey Tent & Event Rentals: Chairs, tables, linens (Friday & Sunday), lighting, silverware, glassware | mahaffeytent.com
Memphis Dawls: Friday night music | thememphisdawls.com
Mimsie Crump: Stylist | mimspettit@hotmail.com
Newman Farm: Berkshire pigs | newmanfarm.com
Propcellar Vintage Rentals: Whiskey barrels, antique doors, quilts, potting stand, courtyard furniture (Saturday night), tea tins (Sunday brunch) | propcellar.com
Side Street Steppers: Sunday brunch music | sidestreetsteppers.com
Small Fires Press: Signature fox logo, cups, towels, napkins, journal | smallfirespress.com
Teresa White: Glass blowing | 901.336.6555
Valerie June: Saturday night music | valeriejune.com
Woodson Ridge Farm: 'Honey Bear', butternut, spaghetti and acorn squash, scarlett queen turnips, 'black beauty' and Japanese eggplant, red choi, dwarf green pac choi, hon tsai tai, 'bright lights' rainbow chard | woodsonridgefarms.com

HEMINGWAY'S TABLE
Holliday Flowers & Events: Vases, lighting, palm trees and fronds| hollidayflowers.com
Lit Restaurant Supply: Carafes | litsupply.com
Mahaffey Tent & Event Rentals: Silverware, glassware, stage | mahaffeytent.com
New Ballet Ensemble: Flamenco performance | newballet.org
Propcellar Vintage Rentals: Vintage furniture, books, typewriters | propcellar.com
Roy Brewer: Guitar performance | 901.282.5460
Spruce: Vases, floral design, event styling | spruceshop.com
Whole Foods: Food purveyor | wholefoodsmarket.com

HOMEGROWN TREASURES
Garden District: Lanterns, floral arrangements, furniture, event styling | gardendistrictmemphis.com
Mahaffey Tent & Event Rentals: Chairs, tables, linens, tent | mahaffeytent.com
Athens Distributing Company: Alcoholic beverages | athensdistributing.com
Farm Truck Organics: Food purveyor | farmtruckorganics.com
Hattiloo Theatre: *Grease* performance | hattiloo.org
Ballet Memphis: *Running Ahead of Fate* performance | balletmemphis.org
Derrick Dent: Artist | derrickdent.com
Jim Spake & Joe Restivo: Music | jimspake.com

FUNKYLUX

Athens Distributing Company: Alcoholic beverages | athensdistributing.com
Augusta Campbell: Stylist | Augustacampbell@comcast.net
The Bo-Keys: Music | thebokeys.com
DJ Witnesse: Disc jockey | jason@thinkhead.com
Flashback Memphis: Vintage shirts | flashbackmemphis.com
Holliday Flowers & Events: Centerpieces, flowers, microphone bar, lighting | hollidayflowers.com
Mahaffey Tent & Event Rentals: Tables, chairs, linens, silverware, plates, glasses, outdoor kitchen | mahaffeytent.com
Whole Foods: Food purveyor | wholefoodsmarket.com
http://www.foodterms.com/encyclopedia/olive-oil/index.html

NAPA CHIC

Cornerstone Cellars and Stepping Stone Cellars: Wines | cornerstonecellars.com
Garden District: Lanterns, floral arrangements | gardendistrictmemphis.com
Farm Truck Organics: Food purveyor | farmtruckorganics.com
Kate Bradley: Portraits | katebradleyfineart.com
Mahaffey Tent & Event Rentals: Table, chairs, silverware, glassware | mahaffeytent.com
Shindigs by Sheril: Chargers, menu design, party favor concept, event styling | shindigsbysheril.com
Tennessee Shakespeare Company: Shakespeare performance | tnshakespeare.org

SAVORY SOUTH

Buster's Liquors & Wines: Alcoholic beverages | bustersliquors.com
Farm Truck Organics: Food purveyor | farmtruckorganics.com
Garden District: Floral arrangements, lighting, menu, event styling | gardendistrictmemphis.com
Randall Andrews: Garage kitchen art | deltadebris@gmail.com
Veritas Glass: Glassware | veritasglass.com
Voices of the South: *Why I Live at the P.O.* performance | voicesofthesouth.org

SING FOR YO SUPPA

Athens Distributing Company: Alcoholic beverages | athensdistributing.com
Emma Lincoln: Pies | ourmotherstable.com
Holliday Flowers & Events: Tree lighting, floral arrangements | hollidayflowers.com
Mahaffey Tent & Event Rentals: Silverware, glassware, lighting, stage, Tuscan tables and chairs, linens | mahaffeytent.com
Marcella Simien + Her Lovers: Music performance | swampsoulbooking@gmail.com
Metal Museum Store | metalmuseum.org
Terrance Simien: Special musical guest | terrancesimien.com
Wayne Edge: Sculptures | davidluskgallery.com/artists/wayne.edge
Whole Foods: Food purveyor | wholefoodsmarket.com

VINTAGE AMERICANA

Amurica Photo Booth: Photographs | amurica.com
Buster's Liquors & Wines: Alcoholic beverages | bustersliquors.com
Farm Truck Organics: Food purveyor | farmtruckorganics.com
Indie Memphis: Film projection | indiememphis.org
JJ Keras: Stylist | jjkeras@gmail.com
Kait Lawson: Music performance | madjackrecords.com
Mahaffey Tent & Event Rentals: Silverware, glassware, lighting, stage | mahaffeytent.com
Muddy's Bake Shop: Desserts | muddysbakeshop.com
Propcellar Vintage Rentals: Potting stand, quilts, phonograph, vintage furniture | propcellar.com

WATCH YO HED

Athens Distributing Company: Alcoholic beverages | athensdistributing.com
Blind Mississippi Morris: Music performance | ramentertainment.com
Eden Brent: Music performance | edenbrent.com
Farm Truck Organics: Food purveyor | farmtruckorganics.com
Garden District: Floral arrangements, candles, lanterns, events | gardendistrictmemphis.com
Mahaffey Tent & Event Rentals: Tables, chairs, silverware, plates, glassware, linens, lighting | mahaffeytent.com
Propcellar Vintage Rentals: Mattress spring | propcellar.com
Project: Motion: Dance performance | projectmotiondance.org
Ray & Baudoin Interior Design: Chandeliers, event styling | rb-id.com

WOMEN IN CAMO 2014

Founded in 2010 by Tommie Dunavant, Women in Camo is a unique group of women who support Conservation Through Art and Wildy Abundant. Their enthusiasm for the sporting life is contagious, and they are truly an inspiration. With each of their memberships they are also supporting *MEMPHIS: Sweet, Spicy & a Little Greasy.*

Connie Adams	Jane-Kathryn Evans	Maggie Phillips
Kathryn Asmus	Marsha Evans	Selden Popwell
Caroline Billups	Liz Farnsworth	Carol Prentiss
Anne Bobo	Elizabeth Gillespie	Melissa Rainer
Sophia Bollinger	Lucia F. Gilliland	Amy Rhodes
Elizabeth Brown	Amy Birdsong Golden	Shade Robinson
Lisa Brown	Harriet Goshorn	Beth Rouse
Beth R. Buffington	Martha Hester	Elizabeth Rouse
Alice R. Burnett	Eva Hussey	Leslie Rouse
Lisa Buser	Barbara Hyde	Diane Rudner
Meg Clifton	Susan Inman	Sally D. Saig
Kate Connell	Sandra Jones	Susan Schadt
Rhea Crenshaw	Anne Orgill Keeney	Lila L. Sessums
Senter C. Crook	Kathy Ledbetter	Jane Slatery
Sherrill M. Crump	Susan Lee	Nancy Smith
Lindsey Roberts Daniels	Lisa May	Susan Smith
Cindy Dobbs	Janie Lowery	Brooke H. Sparks
Katherine Dobbs	Emily McEvoy	Anne Stokes
Anne Dunavant	Linda Milbrandt	Mary Katherine Stout
Jennifer Pierotti Dunavant	Ellen Miller	Stephanie D. Tancredi
Kelli Dunavant	Ann Morgan	Mary Seay Taylor
Leslie Dunavant	Musette S. Morgan	Kate Thakkar
Michelle Dunavant	Snow Morgan	Pat Kerr Tigrett
Tommie Dunavant	Nancy Morrow	Muffy Turley + The Scout Guide Memphis
Livia Dunklin	Dianne Papasan	Anna Wunderlich

INDEX

www.wildabundancepublishing.com

Published in 2014 by
ArtsMemphis
575 South Mendenhall
Memphis, Tennessee 38117
www.artsmemphis.org

Photographs © Wild Abundance Publishing
All photos by Lisa Buser

Text and design © 2014 ArtsMemphis
Designed by Susan Schadt

Library of Congress cataloging-in-publication
data available

ISBN 978-0-692-24204-9

Printed in the United States by

WIMMER
cookbooks
wimmerco.com   800.548.2537
AN RR DONNELLEY COMPANY
"Cookbooks of Distinction"™